BLUE DUST

Ayesha Salman is a writer and poet. Her poems have been published in several literary journals in the UK including *Smoke* and *Splizz*. She is currently working on two more works of fiction and remains committed to experimental fiction and the complex relationship between private and public domains in terms of meaning and comprehension. She also continues to write poetry. This is her first novel. Ayesha Salman works as a writer and editor in the development sector in Pakistan.

OTHER INDIAINK TITLES

Anjana Basu	*Black Tongue*
Anjana Basu	*Chinku and the Wolfboy*
Anjum Hasan	*Neti, Neti*
A.N.D. Haksar	*Madhav & Kama: A Love Story from Ancient India*
Boman Desai	*Servant, Master, Mistress*
Chitra Banerjee Divakaruni	*Shadowland*
Claudine Le Tourneur d'Ison	*Hira Mandi*
C.P. Surendran	*An Iron Harvest*
Haider Warraich	*The Auras of the Jinn*
I. Allan Sealy	*The Everest Hotel*
I. Allan Sealy	*Trotternama*
Indrajit Hazra	*The Garden of Earthly Delights*
Jaspreet Singh	*17 Tomatoes: Tales from Kashmir*
Jawahara Saidullah	*The Burden of Foreknowledge*
John MacLithon	*Hindutva, Sex & Adventure*
Kalpana Swaminathan	*The Page 3 Murders*
Kalpana Swaminathan	*The Gardener's Song*
Kamalini Sengupta	*The Top of the Raintree*
Madhavan Kutty	*The Village Before Time*
Pankaj Mishra	*The Romantics*
Paro Anand	*Pure Sequence*
Rakesh Satyal	*Blue Boy*
Rani Dharker	*Anurima*
Ranjit Lal	*Black Limericks*
Ranjit Lal	*The Small Tigers of Shergarh*
Ranjit Lal	*The Simians of South Block and Yumyum Piglets*
Raza Mir & Ali Husain Mir	*Anthems of Resistance: A Celebration of Progressive Urdu Poetry*
Sanjay Bahadur	*The Sound of Water*
Shandana Minhas	*Tunnel Vision*
Selina Sen	*A Mirror Greens in Spring*
Sharmistha Mohanty	*New Life*
Shree Ghatage	*Brahma's Dream*
Sudhir Thapliyal	*Crossing the Road*
Susan Visvanathan	*Something Barely Remembered*
Susan Visvanathan	*The Visiting Moon*
Susan Visvanathan	*The Seine at Noon*

FORTHCOMING TITLES

Tanushree Podder	*Escape from Harem*
Greta Rana	*Hidden Women*

BLUE DUST

Ayesha Salman

IndiaInk
ROLI BOOKS

First published in 2012
IndiaInk
An imprint of
Roli Books Pvt. Ltd
M-75, Greater Kailash II Market
New Delhi 110 048
Phone: ++91 (011) 4068 2000
Fax: ++91 (011) 2921 7185
E-mail: info@rolibooks.com; Website: www.rolibooks.com

Also at
Bangalore, Chennai & Mumbai

Cover Design: Sanchita Jain

ISBN: 978-81-86939-64-2

Typeset in Arno Pro by Roli Books Pvt. Ltd
and printed at IBH Printers, Noida

For my mother,
Najma

A green breeze sweeps us up,
In slow mornings of dazzling jasmine,
Waking us to red grass
Sliding beneath our feet.

We live in the shade,
You and I
The cold white light between us.

1

Zaib's Return

As she wiped the trickle of blood from her right thigh, she looked up anxiously to make sure Asad wasn't looking. Within a second, before he could light his next cigarette, she was gone. She disappeared, following the trail of that great big voice of a woman who seemed to be speaking just to her... Alya could now see the woman's large black eyes fixed sternly on the terrified lot in front of her. She looked at them as if she had just fed them their last meal; henceforth they would begin their walk to the afterlife, cleansed and fat with new knowledge and forced devotion. They were immobile, in the middle of a bleeding silence that spread rapidly, filling horror into the hearts of a crowd she was so intimate with today, but hadn't even known the day before. The woman who held the power started to walk away, her huge veil sweeping the floor behind her, her egg-head bursting through the black. The rest were not being able to focus on anything in particular, trying desperately to imagine life again. The living-dead dispersed slowly. They hardly had the strength to drag themselves out of the room. Life wouldn't be the same again... they would live in a self-mutilating state of somnambulism... and Alya felt dirty too, just like them. Dirty, polluted, and damned. She was soiled – soiled with bad blood.

Monsoon dust swirling brick-pink liquid on sidewalks subsumed those that toed the line. In the early hours of the morning, Lahore's ghost life swept through the streets like a phantom, a distant sun lost in the crowd's single anticipatory ache. A faint mist anchored the movements of pedestrians as sheets of rain sank into their clothes. Wax-faced blue crow sitting in an alcove under a chopped-up building shook its head mechanically from east to west, lapping up the hum of the crowd beneath her. She sized up her next meal from a distance, a small limp piece of a bright orange substance stuck comfortably to the wall of the building that was in the process of being pulled down and therefore on the verge of collapse; it wasn't long before she had flown off with bits of orange pulp hanging from her beak. Finally, she became a small dot lost to the sky.

'Alya, when was the last time you saw your mother? Alya when was it? Was it in hospital or at home? What exactly do you remember?' Probe. Probe. Probe. Nothing, I can't remember anything. Nothing. Nothing, I can't remember anything. Please let me be, just for now, just for one minute.

The words wrapped her up inside them. It hadn't been that long since it happened. But now what? What next? Where will the next part take me? What was ammi going to bring home this time?

'Alya was your mother awake when you saw her. Did she tell you anything about Hassan?' Damn doctors – butchers. Drill. Drill. Drill. *I can't think.*

Alya had been watching the rain for at least an hour from her bedroom window. She looked outside and imagined herself flat naked on her back on the road in front of her, palms balanced on soft baking cement, breasts caressed by the warm folds of air surrounding her. Another decadent monsoon pushing the limits of predictability covered her like a blanket as she tried to rearrange the reckless sky with her eyes. A steady trickle of water bubbles streaking the glass in front of her lulled her into a forced sense of serenity. For a second there was nothing... just water and air.

She gazed at the pedestrians, running for shelter; a dissipating jigsaw secluded by its surroundings. She marveled at how stark the world looked, washed by the rain, stripped to the bone. Tiny droplets of water bounced off the road deliciously like millions of small crystals. She had a sudden urge to run outside and bathe in the rain like she used to with her sister when she was a child, spinning round and round in circles until she would finally fall down dizzy, dripping with water. She became aware of those in front of her scuttling from place to place, each trying to get to their destination, each locked in a reverie about how the day ahead will unfold, busy with thoughts of the predicted events of the next few hours, events that may never even take place; events that were determined by unknown forces scribbling the destinies of millions. How certain we are of ourselves, she thought, in this huge abyss of unknown ends. Who knows what may happen and how far it will take us, perhaps never to return. That's how things happen, in seconds, changing the future course of events forever. She knew how that worked. One step back. One step forward.

Still staring out of the window, her gaze shifted to the grey frothing gutter just outside her gate; she felt dryness at the back of her throat and tasted the bitter stench of feces. The imminent arrival of her mother cut through her. That's why things were topsy-turvy in her head. She had forgotten to take out the rubbish the previous night, despite the mess it had caused in the kitchen. The smell of the earth outside reminded her of something, of some other time when she was a child with chocolate fingers and mud on her mouth. She had asked Zaib, her mother, whether the earth had chocolate in it. Zaib had laughed and kissed her.

'Yes baby there is a whole load of chocolate in the earth! But not the kind you can eat because it is mixed with mud and it's bitter!'

She smiled at her mother's bizarre answers. She was constantly surprising, re-inventing things in her own way. It was mostly annoying at the time. Now it was endearing. And she wanted it back. But over the years much had been left unsaid, unsettled between them. No matter how hard they tried, something had slipped by before its time and they were unable to reclaim it as their own. Her eyes moistened at the thought that Zaib might want to come back and spend some time with her just to be with her. But that was impossible, not after the way they had parted the last time they met. Ammi was not that forgiving; not anymore. She was coming back to reshuffle the cards.

Alya recalled the last time she saw her in Zakar. She was talking incoherently, almost in fragments, to the extent that some of what she said seemed an affectation for Alya's sympathy at best. She was reading *Tender is the Night*.

Zaib kept calling it 'an ice-cream like substance'.

Alya, who had never read the book, looked at her oddly. 'That means nothing ammi. What do you mean?'

That seemed to set ammi off, and the discussion ended in an argument about various unrelated issues from the past, which led to Alya catching the next flight out. Subsequently, they had talked on the phone and it seemed as if things were relatively peaceful between them. But then there was a postcard that had come a month ago. It had a picture of colourless seagulls with a red horizon in the background. The fake lucidity of it made Alya sick and she had the urge to throw it away immediately, as soon as it arrived, unexpectedly, on her doorstep, but the fear of what it might contain compelled her to read it. Ammi's notes usually had fear attached to them. The postcard was short and concise but said nothing of consequence.

Sweetheart,

I have missed you so much. I must see you soon. Please call me, don't worry I am ok, but I have something important to tell you.

See you soon.

I love you meri jaan.

Your mummy.

Why did she always have to be so vague? Was it a deliberate ploy, a cry for attention, just another charade? And why 'mummy'? As far as Alya could recall, she had always called her Ammi. Perhaps she wanted to move back to Lahore. Her throat was dry again. The room she was standing in, her sitting room, bore into her, invisible unused flat strings balancing things without reason – familiar things – now from another place sent a shiver up her spine; they discarded her – tables and chairs, sofas and windows, small nick knacks… a small white porcelain doll. She felt alienated in her own house, there was nowhere to hide, no shelter from ammi.

She wished she had more time. She knew it was simply her fear of what might happen and that, even if she had had another year to try and predict what might or might not conspire in those next few hours, she still wouldn't have had enough time, so when Zaib arrived she was strangely relieved to be much closer to the truth.

Zaib was in a white embroidered *shalwar kameez* and immediately hugged her daughter. Her hair was, as always, disheveled, (they almost looked dust caked), but the red lipstick was still there, matt, like chalk. The eyeliner was shining. She was still so beautiful.

'I see you have redecorated the lounge.' She forced a smile. Her ammi of those earlier days would have had a million suggestions to offer, but this time there was just a crippling silence.

And then came, 'Oh it was a tiring flight but the clouds kept me going!'

A slight wave of the arms and that set Alya off. Alya's head crawled uncomfortably with a thousand images from her childhood... she could hear her mother's thrilled voice, 'Come on children, let's go for a wild long drive!' Everything was an adventure, everything a journey full of surprises exceeding exhilaration. Ammi would always say things in fixed equations as if they were doubtless certainties. On such occasions, Alya and her sister hoped ammi's happiness would stretch unendingly, terrified of what would happen if ammi went home upset. The drive usually took them to the milkshake man at Liberty Market in the heart of the city of Lahore, where they would drink pints of orange milkshake, laughing like puppets at ammi's jokes. A glittering Liberty Market shone with rows and rows of lacey light bulbs that looked like yellow plums. And the mango milkshake man, (best known in the market for the quality of his milkshake), was always dressed in a starched white *shalwar kameez,* his teeth as white as his clothes, a glistening white that lingered like sunshine long after the drive was over. Repeated thoughts of him and his bear hands made Alya nostalgic and she suddenly wished she could be back in her mother's arms, a child without barriers.

The smell of the dripping blood sky outside: sickness overpowered her. She wished again she could be transported somewhere else, now, before it was too late. Her mother looked undistorted, unlike the last head she wore. The creases on her forehead had smoothed out and she had a cold calmness about her that was daunting. The dazed doll-like eyes of Zakar had disappeared and a strange tranquility had set in its place. She had obviously reached a resolution. Alya's fear of the unknown almost choked her. The room, with its now immovable objects, had become absurd.

Zaib smiled her test-tube smile.

'He died four years ago.'

The shadow of a bright white moth prickled her mouth as it flew across the room frantically.

'I have been in my room for the last three months… with no one else.'

What did she want Alya to say? Did she want sympathy, pity?

Alya remembered her mother four years earlier. Her hair is thick with blood. Flies glance at her, just in case. Spit spit spit. The room smells of cheese.

The constant groaning of an old pedestal fan in one corner of the room is a comforting yet sad souvenir from lost time slots in a distant but happier past.

'Why don't you have an AC in this room?'

She always went off on a tangent at the oddest times.

'I can't afford one in every room ammi.' She said it without emotion, but it seemed to disturb Zaib nevertheless.

An unexpected outburst followed, 'That bastard, I will kill him; she can never have him, never!'

The characteristic approval of a mother was required, but the roles could not be reversed.

'Ammi, baba is not with us anymore.'

It had to be said. It was not possible to hide her fear and Zaib picked up on it instantly.

'Do not try and make me look like a fool Alya, I know what you and your father really think of me!'

Alya stood up and swatted the maddening moth, which by now had spread itself across the white tube light as a last attempt to gain a little more life. She watched it flutter until it finally faded making Alya feel even more helpless. The conversation was futile and Alya knew she had to end it somehow. Zaib carried on. She was relentless.

'Alya, how could you break it, it was my favourite vase, my favourite Chinese trophy. Now it is pressed down flat and has no beauty, just lines that don't merge.'

This was going to live beyond her love for her mother. That vase had been in her head for more than fifteen years. How much more would she have to endure, and where were they going to go with all this? She felt a pounding in her head, but for Zaib's sake she had trained her voice to be calm. After all they had both been in a similar place before.

'I am sorry. Do you want to come back home ammi?'

'I have been in therapy,' she said proudly.

'I am glad ammi; it's good for you and necessary of course.'

'Alya don't patronize me.'

Zaib scratched her head, sandpaper skull.

Alya could smell skin.

'He slept with that woman, I know it.'

Alya thought she was losing her grip on reality. Was it real? She saw a pink canary on Zaib's shoulder; butterflies strapped to her feet. The room looked bare and alien.

'Where is baba now?' She wanted to know how much her mother remembered.

'We put him in the river with the blue whale. Before I could save him, he left us.'

'It's not your fault ammi.'

'You have never believed me! You have always been on his side!' A steely silence swept across the room, settling in hidden crevices.

We are an ocean, shhh, quiet ripples in water. Ammi please don't leave me.

Alya took Zaib's hand and helped her get up. They walked slowly to Alya's bedroom where she sat with her mother on the bed, watching her carefully, trying to look in control, trying not to let her know how frightened and abandoned she felt. Zaib reclined against the pillow and fell asleep.

Please don't take her away. She is not dead, just sick, soul sick.

As she sat by her mother, Alya's blue-powder days swept into the room as if ushered in by the wind, caressing her hair with their distant warmth. Where was he now, where was Asad? Was he still waiting for her somewhere, in some secret hideout? He seemed frozen in time, unable to move past history... safe in her memory. Her body ached for him, even after everything that had happened. She wanted *him* to tell her how desirable she was. She wanted *him* to touch her. She wanted him in her bed holding her against his chest. But that was wrong, wasn't it?

But then she had always been the soiled one, the one to be mistrusted, the one who had 'vague morals' or worse 'no morals at all'. The television was on in the next room. Flashes of panic-stricken people running across a road somewhere filled the screen. A bomb had gone off in some big shopping area in the old city of Lahore. The newscaster was straining hard to sound dramatic. But there was no drama to it anymore. Scenes of bits of flesh stuck to sidewalks and distraught mothers dead before their time filled her head like a dye. Death had just become another episode in the lives of the thousands who didn't know where they would wake up the next day, or if indeed they would wake up at all. The smell of the earth, 'her' earth filled her nostrils and she felt there might be hope. Please don't let it happen again…

Ammi twitched. Maybe I should get Amber for her. Ammi loved her dolls, always had.

૧૪૭

She needs air. Whispers, whispers. She pushes through herself and ammi outside and pulls in air. Quickly. Green sky, lop-sided mouth grins. It yops at her. Hurts her pulsating head not to remember where the blue flower is. The one she picked with ammi when she was little. The one ammi loved and kept for years. Her fingers warming silver-spine trees. Bloody ants on the wall, again! Always there. It hurt not to remember, not to remember at all, not for any time at all, if someone had ever told her how long things that were around her had been there before she could remember. Mostly remembering small truths like those tended to confirm her existence. But she has not been told; nobody would tell her and that meant she was stuck on a firm point of non-gratification and non-reversal, in a small place of immovable inequities. Me and me and me, only me. She wanted to wipe herself out somehow so that the entire racket in her head would stop. Once and for all. Sky space slips from her mind and is rapidly replaced by mama's fixed dolls, hanging porcelain – unchanging, crudely. This is fragmenting. Me. My bits stuck here and everywhere. Unlaced porcelain children, glass eyes searing, sucking the life from her, rocking her upside down. They swallow into her; she touches her face. She is nine again – in terror with frills and red marble clothes, cold – cutting her. Still she is worried about ammi. Where is she? Is she safe?

… Pins scrape my head of weeds as I look right and left, left and right, plastic head stuck to me, not mine, such strange inertia in my pulse and the bad bad smell excludes me so I am me and alone and I am me with me.

Ammi are you with me?

૧૪૭

2

Pictures

As the sun set and the rain came to a standstill, a sickly scent of seeping wet roses breezed through the window. Alya looked at her mother anxiously who was still asleep. Her initial anger subsided and was replaced with a raging fear. How long has it been since the doctors had said that Zaib had finally accepted the fact that Hassan had gone? Stories of grinning green gnomes and pink-feathered fairies with starlit eyes and soft hair filled Alya's mind with frightening images, as she tried to re-trace her mother's childhood. She couldn't understand it. There were too many contradictions. She had been working towards wiping out her mother's sadness all her life, but somehow at that moment with her lying helplessly in front of her like a child, she felt it had all come to nothing.

She thought about Zaib's past with its inconsistencies, and about how her own life had been so similar in a way. The pain had been there; it had just originated from a different sore. It was not what she bargained for, but things happen and leave their indelible mark on lives, the lilt of a wave in the ocean that nobody can predict or prevent. She opened the same old photo album she had flicked through so many times before – with pictures of the last three generations of her family, some almost crumbling, others shone of newness as if they had just been placed there though they may have been twenty years old. A fickle memory has remnants too, she thought.

The first picture was one from the first week she, ammi, Sonia, and baba had just moved back to Pakistan from Zakar. She was thirteen. The beginning of the 'honeymoon months' as she thought of them before baba left and before Asad came into her life. She recalled how Devi khala had doted on her, buying her clothes, making her favourite dishes, spoiling her in every way possible. She'd climb into Devi khala's bed at night just because she wanted to tuck her feet between her feet to feel the warmth of her hot-water bottle that always kept the bed so comfortable she never wanted to leave it. It was impossible to know when things had changed or if they had always been like that and she just didn't know about it. That perfect veneer of happiness lasted a while.

She combed Zaib's hair with her fingers. The grey was showing. That's not like ammi, she thought. 'Ammi, are you asleep?' There was just a steady movement of her chest. Alya took a sigh of relief.

She looked at the pictures again trying to find some trace of what was to come in the frozen actors in front of her, an expression, a gesture, a frown, any proof that all that was to follow was real, not just some make-belief life that she had been imagining all this time, but all she saw were expressions of elation, her mother grinning and hugging the sister she loved so much and had missed for so long, keeping her close to her as if this time she would never let go, she and Asad arm in arm, offering their best smiles, Sonia looking peaceful and content, basking in the sun. Where were the signs that she looked for so desperately? Where was the truth? But then such is the nature of pictures; they are like a hallucination made to fit a feeling, an emotion, an image carved out of a dream. They are simply pictures of a lost time, the beauty of a thought that we design to cover up the ashes beneath.

She fixed her gaze on Asad, her Devi khala's eldest son. He looked so vivacious and energetic, as if he would come out of the picture now and whisk her away to some distant land of love and adventure. After all that had transpired between them, he still looked as if he could fix anything. She could almost hear him saying, 'Come on sweetheart smile for me, I won't have you look so gloomy, *chal chalen* (come on let's go), let's do something more exciting!'

Despite everything, she still couldn't help feeling that Asad would have been so different had he had it easier. A rush of memories came to her so unexpectedly that they brought with them a flood of tears and she buried her face in her hands, hiding herself in her palms while she re-traced her life at that time. She tried hard to focus on what really happened. She instinctively looked back at Zaib who was still fast asleep. Ammi could never know.

She went back to Asad's difficult childhood, just as she had so many times before – to his life before her. Asad was boyish looking even as a man, he had curly hair that shone different shades of brown in the sun and he had a particular twinkle in his eye, a glint that survived his childhood and gave him the aura of someone who was friendly and easy going, someone who tended to look at the brighter side of life. But as a teenager he became moody and opinionated, burying himself in the books of the great philosophers, Descartes, Nietzsche, Plato and others. He would emerge as a Muslim fanatic and then just as suddenly a hard-nosed atheist. His prism head perplexed her and fascinated her.

When she moved back to Pakistan with her parents she was oblivious of the details of events in Devi's or in Asad's life in the few years preceding their return. Zaib was strangely private about her relationship with Devi, almost as if it was sacred. She had never really discussed her sister in much detail with her daughters. All Alya knew was that Devi khala was having some problems with her husband. Even for the first few months after her arrival in Pakistan, she had no idea what those problems were and Devi seemed perfectly happy and well settled to her.

But she noticed that something had changed about Asad this time. She couldn't work out what was wrong exactly. He seemed more somber and morose. He had always been lively and uplifting, making everyone laugh and cracking inane jokes at the most inopportune moments. But this time he had changed. He would slip into a darker mood, losing himself in his own thoughts, separating himself from the rest. In an odd way it made him more mysterious to Alya and she wanted to delve deeper, to try and unravel what was inside. She once saw a new scar on his forehead and asked him what it was.

'Oh, it is just a gash from a fist fight with one of the boys.'

'Do you have lots of those kinds of fights?'

'No,' he smiled, 'only when it is necessary.'

Alya admired the way he said it with such nonchalance as if it was a common occurrence. She also admired his clothes and what they stood for, the crisp starched *shalwar kameez* and *kusas* he always wore; he said he had no time for western clothes or western ideologies and that he had finally abandoned all western philosophies to embrace Islam. 'I have read all those philosophies and it is obvious that they have been designed to deflect us from the truth, the truth of God.' He'd sometimes stare hard into her eyes and cover her head with her *dupatta*, tucking the sides behind her ears and smile, 'You look so innocent.' He'd pinch her cheek, almost exactly like her father sometimes did.

She admired the intelligent way in which he spoke about religion and philosophy, and he enjoyed sharing his ideas and readings with her. She was ten years younger, but she was bright too and understood a lot of what he said. He, on the other hand, had the patience to explain concepts to her and enjoyed being indulged by her. Over the following months, Alya started spending more time with him. Initially, she simply felt animated in his company, but gradually she realized that every time she was about to meet him or go to his house, her heart would start beating faster and she would feel an odd rush of excitement in her stomach. She couldn't understand it at first, but with time the feeling became more intense. She started to feel embarrassed by the strange new emotions that fed on her, growing all the time, multiplying inside her as they became harder to hide. She hoped he couldn't detect anything, *anything that would be really embarrassing.*

It was a Sunday. She was sure of that.

Ammi, Alya, and Sonia are sleeping over at Devi's. It is late at night. Everyone except Alya is fast asleep. She is distracted by thoughts of Asad and she keeps getting up and looking out of the window. The sky is clear. Hundreds of stars puncture the flat black night and the full moon looks frail like tissue.

She is suddenly interrupted by someone at the door and before she can walk over and check who it is, she hears the creak of the door.

'Who is it?' she whispers, slightly scared. She senses it is him. Oh God, oh no he knows!

'Asadbhai, is it you?'

'Yes it's me, I can't sleep.'

'That's weird, neither can I.'

'If you want to talk, you can come into my room, the lights are on in there. We won't disturb anyone.'

Her heart seems to miss a beat.

She slips out of the room quietly and into Asad's.

ཙ

Which day should I pick to step on a life? Will it make a difference whether it's a Sunday or Saturday, July or June, sunny or cold? ... The salt breeze of Zakar's beaches washed over her face.

ཙ

3

Mummy and Daddy

I wish I could kill her. She thinks she knows everything and she tries to tell me what is right and wrong, I hate the way she acts like some kind of God ... I saw mummy getting dressed for the hospital this morning, she looked so beautiful, I pray to God that one day I am like her... Thursday 3 September

There was no year. She wished it was there. It must have been after Devi left, she thought.

Alya had read many parts of Zaib's diary; strangely, the entries in her diary were full of contradictions with reference to her mother. Alya had read some of them when she was clearing up her things from the old family house in Gulberg that Zaib sold before the family left for Zakar. But where was her father in all this, where did he fit in? He wasn't really mentioned much at all.

Zaib's father, Shafi, had been a renowned lawyer in Pakistan; he was part of the elite of Lahore. Shafi had carved a niche for himself at a young age through sheer hard work and determination. He was always ambitious and had told his father, 'One day I will make it big' and he had proved it. From a poor Muslim family, he had put himself through college, by doing night shifts in a steel factory. His father, a respected teacher in a local school, struggled to support his family of seven with his modest income. His mother, a housewife with five children, had learnt to endure the hardships of poverty over the years and remained a dedicated and supportive wife and mother. Similar to the *obedient and dutiful* wife Shafi would later marry.

Shafi had continued to help support his parents during their lifetime and he still sent money to some of his poorer, less fortunate relatives, relatives who were less talked about in the houses of the upper echelons of Pakistani society. He worked hard during the week, often coming home late at night. Zaib would ask him about his work and he would do his best to answer her often-complicated questions.

'I try and teach bad people a lesson so that they don't do wrong things, like lying, cheating and stealing.'

'But daddy, what if they don't listen and they do it again?'

'They do listen because once they are punished for their crimes they know that if they do it again they will be punished again.'

'But what if they are not scared of punishments?'

Zaib's father was constantly reminded of Zaib's intelligence and her fiercely independent way of thinking. He remembered when Zaib had barely started speaking, one of her first questions to him was, 'Daddy who made us?' When he replied, 'God', she asked, 'Who made God?' When she was a little older, she came running to him after school once, terrified, saying that she had heard someone telling the children that there were many Gods and many lives that each of us have to live through over and over again. 'Daddy, they said that we can even be born as snails or ants. Does that mean one day I will become an ant?'

He was amused and marveled at this bright star, this feisty little girl, who dissected everything that came her way like an adept surgeon, hungry for more knowledge and new discoveries, trying constantly to uncover the secrets of the world. She challenged him intellectually even as a child and he admired her for it.

Zaib's mother, a medical doctor, was a woman of few words. She was seen by many as unemotional and cold and often found extreme display of emotion uncomfortable and unnecessarily dramatic. She often called Zaib, 'our drama queen,' or even more annoyingly for Zaib, 'our little actress'. Zaib found that belittling even as a child. When she had her own children, she would tell her daughters, 'That is exactly what I don't want to do to you, sum you up in a few choice words. She summed me up as if she were diagnosing a disease or writing a damn prescription.'

Shafi tended to his garden on the weekends. It was his way of relaxing. He tilled the soil for hours, planting new saplings and flowers, plucking fresh green vegetables from his vegetable garden, marveling at the perfect shapes and tiny nuances of each vegetable and fruit, every tiny mottled bud and flower.

'Look Zaib, look at that aubergine, what a perfect purple it is, like a big planet in the sky.'

He would walk around in chopped jeans and a white *kurta*, patting his sunshine belly from time to time, in a satisfied manner, studying and scrutinizing the leaves of his trees and plants individually as if he were reading some story inscribed on each of the great creations of nature. Zaib could picture him in later years holding a leaf between his fingers delicately, frowning with concentration, a blend of tenderness and fascination in his eyes. 'My father saw a world in each thing,' she would say to people about him after he had gone. Zaib kept close to her father on these occasions trying to learn about the secrets of her garden from daddy, trying to find the same peace he seemed to discover in his world of little wonders. Those enchanting childhood mornings that filled her nostrils with the scent of honey and hot toast were to her, heaven on earth. Daddy would wake up soon after the birds. First he prayed then watered his plants in the garden. The dark wrinkled mango trees, which he had spent years nurturing, spoke to Zaib softly and tenderly so that even the fetus mango knew who she was. Zaib could hear the murmuring secrets of his trees and plants even after he'd died. 'The beauty of a tree is in its birth and its death. When a tree is born *again* it is even more beautiful,' he would say. Sometimes Zaib couldn't help feeling left out when he was with his plants and trees so she would break their leaves when she thought she was being ignored; daddy pretended not to notice.

But her happiness would be short-lived and though she tried to squeeze as much out of those few hours as she could, she knew the weekends would inevitably turn sour. She could not remember the last time her parents could spend more than half an hour together without arguing. The weekends meant neither of her parents could escape from each other. As far as Zaib was concerned, it was her mother who was usually to blame and it generally happened after one of mummy's shopping sessions. Zaib dreaded those damned shopping sprees because it meant that she would be bought things she hated and she would have to meet her unsavoury, ugly-hearted khalas, who would inevitably upset her and usually her father too. In general it involved all three of her khalas, who like her mother were shopaholics.

The shopping days were always a time of great excitement for her mother, measured by yards of silk, chiffon, or cotton. Zaib often wondered why the material mattered so much. Her mother would force Zaib to go with her to the clothes shops in the most obscure places far from the city and buy floral prints that she despised, so that they could be made into 'pretty' *shalwar kameezs* or worse still billowing dresses for her to wear.

At first Zaib had tried to complain and even resist but soon she gave up because her mother would glare at her so severely, she wouldn't dare question her aesthetics again. It was also because she knew mother brought things up again and again and that was something she wanted to avoid at all cost. After shopping all day her mother always telephoned her three sisters and invited them over for dinner. Zaib would also be summoned to join them. The conversations were the same every time. Zaib related those stories to Alya when Alya was a child as if they were happening as she spoke, conjuring up the images as she talked, gesticulating wildly.

'My mother would be at her *arooj* (zenith) when she saw her sisters, they were everything for her.' This would happen every time they arrived.

She would go on to paint the scene for Alya vividly.

'Ruksana would invariably come up with, "Oh *apa* they are breathtaking!" She would touch the material as if tasting it." The rich fabric would be all around her drowning her like an ocean.'

'Mother would eventually end up offering half of what she had bought to them.'

'And it was always Bilquees who would try to resist, "*Apa*, we really can't." And look at her other two sisters, "How can we?" But it was never a question.'

Zaib would almost carve the images out of thin air and talk about them all as if they were right there, right now.

'Sheila, "Let me see how this one looks against the tone of my skin ... "Rakshi (Ruksana's pet name) pass me the pink, thank you, oh I like this one too." She doesn't have enough hands and the excitement is rising in her voice. I can almost see the saliva on her ugly round chin! By this time mother would resemble a dolphin basking in the sun. The fusion of various expensive perfumes would turn the air to lead and my head would start to feel like a rock.'

'Mother would say after a few minutes, "Well I think you must have it." And that too would be given away.'"

'Then Esther, the maid who cleaned the house would bring the cards.'

Zaib would go on and on, pouring out the images one by one, but Alya had little understanding as a child of how much all of it had affected her mother. Sometimes she'd tell her stories in the present tense like the story she told Alya when Alya was about ten years old.

'She has a small rusty metal box which jingles with one paisa coins and which she opens with increasing relish as the years wear on and cards become more and more imbedded in her life. They play bridge for what seems like five or six hours and then they finally leave but they wouldn't leave without first saying a few well chosen words to me, such as "Oh Zaib you look so frail *beta*, not eating well?" or "Your mother tells us you are not getting top marks in school, no slipping in your studies ok, you know your cousins are all top of their classes."'

From what Zaib had told Alya, after they'd leave, at some late hour of the evening mother would routinely take off her glasses and rub her eyes. Zaib would be relieved that the 'witches', as she and her sister Devi called them, had left, but something even worse would usually follow. This was a time of great fear for Zaib because it meant her parents were alone and it made her think of the plague in England with red crosses on the doors of the diseased (she had read about it at school in her history books. When she asked one of her teachers about the plague the teacher said that white people had been cursed for being heathens and failing to follow the word of God. It was the first sign of hell, *dauzak*, she said. People like that teacher often told Zaib *kayamat* was close – either because people did not have enough faith or because it was the wrong 'type' of faith that they were following.) Somehow she associated her parents' arguments with the feeling of horror that the thought of the plague brought out in her.

Her mother would usually start with, 'How much money have you given *them* this time?'

'How many times do I have to tell you, whatever I give them is the minimum requirement of the court is, please keep your voice down, the children are listening.' His shoulder stooped and his hands reaching out to her for mercy. (So were the cook – listening – and the maids and the sweeper).

'Do not lie to me, you liar! You give those children a lot more than they need and your first responsibility is to this family!'

Those children? *His* children.

Mother lies: mother medusa *and* her womb bed.

It inevitably ended up with Shafi asking her for forgiveness and Zaib wondering why daddy always gave in to her. How could a man who could be so strong with the world, be so weak in his own house?

After her daddy's trial, as she thought of it, Zaib would sit at his bedside while he slept, watching his chest for several minutes in case he stopped breathing. She wished she could take away his troubles but her mother was severe in her unending punishments. She taunted her father about something almost everyday and it was usually connected to *his* family. When Zaib asked him why he didn't stop mummy from shouting at him he said it was because he loved her too much. Zaib knew about love, but she couldn't understand how it could be that bad too, how it could take so much away from a person.

Daddy explained to her, 'You don't understand your mother, you are still very young.' That used to *really* enrage her. At other times he looked sad and said he had to do his duty. She felt sorry for her father for she knew he was defenseless, he just couldn't change, no matter how hard he tried.

She watched him closely, imagining calm seabeds in the wrinkles on his face. For a time she thought everything her father said and did was true and wise. It became her mission to teach his wisdom to others and she tried to make others think his thoughts. Every night she ran her fingers through his grey wispy hair adoringly, doting on his every feature until he would fall into a peaceful sleep. Sometimes she fell asleep next to him until her mother came and woke her up in the middle of the night to take her to her own room. Mother slept in another room as was often customary in those days. Then, one day, daddy told her she was too big to sleep in his room any more and she cried so much she could hardly breathe. Her father didn't realize it would upset her so much and he hugged her tightly, 'Zaib you just wouldn't be comfortable because you are so tall now? Look, what a big girl you are,' but she knew it was more than that, it was a turning point for her – she would no longer be daddy's baby, his little girl. She was being forced to grow up. There was an odd pain in her chest whenever she thought of that day. But daddy tried to make up for it; he still had many stories to tell her before she left him for the night. She made him repeat stories again and again, especially the one about how he met mummy. She loved reminiscing about this 'great' love that existed between her parents before she was born. It was her proof that she was born out of love and not hatred.

'Dad, when she looked at you and smiled, what did you think?'

'I thought, I am a very lucky man and soon after that I asked her to marry me.'

'Did she say yes immediately?'

'Actually, she said yes after a few days, although I know she really wanted to straight away. Who can resist a handsome man like me, ha?'

Zaib's father had met her mother when he was forty. He was already married with three children. After his divorce and his marriage to Zaib's mother, he had started paying alimony to his first wife. Her mother who had married him well aware of everything, still resented his first family and never let him forget about the 'sin' that he had committed, always impressing upon him that his loyalty should first be to 'them', his second, 'more important' family. Even as a child, Zaib knew this was unfair and only once during her childhood had she met her stepsister and brother, something that would cause her great pain in later years.

Zaib knew that her father had had to face great opposition when he decided to get divorced and remarry; something that was unheard of in those days.

'Daddy, were the people of that time horrible to you because no one was supposed to marry again in *those* days?'

Zaib had heard relatives talk about daddy's first marriage and about mummy being a 'Christian'. That had apparently made it *even* worse for him.

'No they weren't, they just misunderstood me and they were not ready for such a big change. You know Zaib big changes only come with the suffering of hundreds of people, sometimes thousands for generations. I did something much smaller in comparison and I think when you fight for something new, in the beginning it is always hard and people misunderstand you until you show them how important change is through your actions.'

'How dad, how did they misunderstand?' She asked perplexed.

He said they did not know, but that he was not meant to be with his first wife, that it was a decision that was ordained. It was in his 'fate' to marry Zaib's mother. 'Your mother and I were destined to be together, just like you and the man you will love and marry.'

'If you were destined to be married, how is it that you married auntie Fatima then, weren't you destined to marry her too?'

'Maybe I was only supposed to be with her for a short time. There must be some reason for that that only God knows about. We don't know everything you know Zaib otherwise we would be God.'

This time, Zaib was thoughtful for a minute and then daddy was gone. The matchstick men crept up to her – for the first time. She saw daddy leaving her mummy and her because God was telling him to, God was saying daddy was not meant to be with them anymore. Suddenly it occurred to her that no matter what she did, her life was not in her control. Destiny controlled *everything*. Daddy was calling out to her.

She was crying. 'Dad, I don't think God wants you to leave us.'

'Of course not.' He hugged her, 'I will never leave my Zaib.'

After her fears had subsided somewhat she touched daddy's cheek and prayed quietly, to herself. She tried to imagine how brave her father must have been to face so much all on his own. But even though she was young she started to carry a strange fear of abandonment within her. Maybe daddy would leave them too; maybe he wouldn't be able to help it. Maybe if he believed strongly enough he would find a new path.

In the mornings, after breakfast, honey and toast with a pint of milk, daddy got dressed for court. She watched him with admiration as he wore his suit and slung his robe on his arm. 'Do you wear a wig everyday in court, dad?'

'Only when my bald patch looks particularly prominent so people take me more seriously.'

'Can I come to court one day and watch you fight?'

'It is not a bull fight you know, although at times I guess you could call it that.'

'Dad, stop it. I want to be with you. Can I come?'

'One day you will but be careful, they might put you in jail thinking you are the offender!'

Zaib enjoyed those coloured moments with her father, but somehow she knew that something important in her house was slowly fading, something was leaving them all. The distant memory of her parents' 'great' love story lingered for a time, but over the decades the mansion she lived in became a somber reminder that love can die. Her father's mango gardens consumed the slow decay of the house that gave birth to phantoms. She thought she would have to wait a long time before she was comfortably warm: but she was stuck right in the middle of the *matchstick men,* mummy and daddy.

ᦃ

4

Zaib's Two Halves

Zaib grew up with two halves, 'the clean half' and the 'dirty half', sometimes the 'clean half' became the 'dirty half' sometimes the 'dirty half' the 'clean half'; it all depended on where she was. Just like the two ends of a rope that look the same but aren't. At school it was her *Christian* half, which was the 'dirty half'. But even outside school, '*Churey*' (the filthy people) was a common name for Christians and she was one of them. The Christians were usually employed as domestic servants; generally sweepers or road cleaners and they were often avoided and spoken to with derision. It was a widely accepted fact that Christians were intrinsically dirtier than Muslims and in most households they were not even allowed to use the same utensils or cutlery. One day Zaib was talking to one of the cleaners in the school and a classmate of hers turned to another and said, 'Look at her talking to them as if they were her own, well then what do you expect they are her own after all, aren't they?' They both laughed and hastily moved away from Zaib and then one of them added, 'Have you noticed, they have a peculiar smell that makes them stand out?'

Zaib's mother was from a staunch Catholic family and although she herself did not attend Mass regularly or read the Bible at home, she always wore a gold cross around her neck as a symbol of her commitment to her religion and contrary to the custom, had refused to covert to Islam when she had married Zaib's father. She had said she refused to succumb to the hypocrisies of society, something about her mother Zaib admired when she had grown up, when she understood better. As a child all she wanted was acceptance. Shafi had initially tried to persuade her to convert, justifying himself by saying that it would make it easier for everyone, 'It's just to keep their mouths shut, and what does it matter to us anyway *jaani*.' 'It matters to me. It's about principles. I love you and that's all that's important, those who can't accept it shouldn't bother meeting us.' As a result many of the friends they had before they became a couple started avoiding them, and their daughters were often derided both by the Muslims and the Christians: they became the untouchables.

Zaib had told her mother about the incessant abuse and taunts she had to listen to day after day at school. Her mother had said she must be strong and learn to 'rise above them' and see through their small mindedness. Zaib understood what she was trying to tell her, but compared to what she had to endure it seemed far less important and most of the time all she wanted was to be just like the other children. Day after day, she was subjected to different kinds of verbal abuse. She was told she was 'black like a Christian and ugly like a Christian' that she stank, that she dressed 'like a Christian', and that she 'was dumb and stupid'. By the time she was in secondary school she had started believing she was dirtier than the other girls and somehow less human. She washed her hands constantly, trying to make them fairer and cleaner. She stared in the mirror and tried to make expressions, such a spouting her lips, to make herself look prettier. She admired popular students and wondered what it would be like to be one of them and looked at them in awe as if they were creatures of another world. She dreaded the summer because she thought no matter how much deodorant she used she would still stink; after all there was something intrinsically wrong with the way she was made. She remembered several occasions when she stood in queues and was told by one or the other student how much she 'stank'.

'Er, Zaib you stink, stay away from me!'

She would shrink away with shame.

For Zaib's sister Devi the taboo of being a Christian woman's daughter was less severe. Being five years older than Zaib, Devi was from an earlier generation when girls were dressed in *burkas* from the moment they attained puberty. Devi spent her teenage years in a black *burka*. At school the girls were less critical of her as she seemed to have the habits and mannerisms of a true *Muslim* girl, keeping herself covered and at least outwardly adhering to the true teachings of Islam. But mainly it was the fact that during her teenage years, her father was rich and influential, and even those who knew his wife was a Christian kept it within their quiet circles as a *known* secret only to be discussed amongst the closest of friends. He was a powerful man and certainly not to be messed with. But by the time Zaib was of the same age, her father had 'fallen from grace' so to speak.

The government had changed and the new military ruler was, according to her father 'a dictator and a butcher'. Public hangings became common place, influential businessmen and politicians disappeared overnight, military officers were given huge mansions to live in, big cars to drive, and their children received the most expensive education the country could offer. Corruption was at its peak, no one knew what would happen next or who would be the next target and the country was gripped with fear. Amidst all the violence and turmoil, a local government official, the Education Secretary's son was abducted and later killed. His body was found ten days later rotting on the banks of the river Ravi. There was enough evidence to suggest that it happened as a result of an old enmity in the family, a political murder. An arrest was made and the case was given to Shafi. On the first night of the hearing he received a phone call directly from the Army Headquarters, telling him that he was ordered to give up the case immediately on the grounds that he did not have enough evidence to convict. The voice on the other end of the phone had said, 'Please understand that this is not a small matter. The man you have captive is from an influential family and we have orders that he be released as soon as possible, it is causing immense inconvenience to a lot of important people, your cooperation will be highly appreciated.'

Shafi had refused to comply and shortly afterwards he was forced to resign. Once again, as in the beginning of his career he had to settle for scraps; small cases thrown his way from old contacts or the few friends he still had. Most of the cases paid poorly and on many occasions he was literally forced to beg for his fee. Sometimes he'd queue up for hours waiting to see a particular client or to collect a cheque, which would end up barely paying the bills.

He felt like he was fresh out of college again, but the difference was that when he was fresh out of college, this was what he was meant to be doing. He was young and it was his time to make a place for himself, but he had done all of that. He had made a place for himself, in fact he had reached the greatest heights of his profession, dined with the most important people in the country, been invited to the homes of ambassadors and foreign politicians, spent afternoons drinking Scotch at the most exclusive local gentlemen's clubs, with former presidents and some of the greatest political and legal minds of the country. But just like that, as if a whole lifetime of work had been obliterated in seconds, it had all gone. His ambition, his work, his dreams suddenly felt unreal, distant and hazy, as if he had never been there, everything seemed like an exercise in futility and it killed a part of him, a part of him that could never recover again. He and his wife were no longer welcome in *high-class* society of Lahore's elite. Shafi gradually became more solitary, preferring to spend hours in his study reading or tending to his garden. Zaib would never forgive them, those vultures that she could pluck out of their opulent homes and kill, one by one. Despite the private hell she was living through, she was so worried about her father's increasing reclusiveness that she couldn't share with him how bad things were at school. She tended to keep her problems to herself sensing that her father was slipping into some dangerous place, something she might not be able to pull him out of.

It was six in the evening on a Sunday. She still remembered it clearly. Her mother came to her. 'I have the perfect solution. A convent.' What did that mean? Mother had decided to send her to a convent about a hundred miles from home. She told her father, 'The education is much better in a convent... plus Zaib is not happy here, she seems to be slipping in her studies. Maybe she needs a change and a new place will do her good and its one of the best in the country.' He had agreed reluctantly and it was finally settled. Zaib was to be sent to the Convent of Jesus and Mary.

Zaib had never learnt much about Christianity; she didn't know its basic tenants and imagined she would be facing a huge statue of Jesus in a big hall with nothing to say to him and no one to guide her about how to pray. But she had no choice. She had to get away to a place where she could keep her sanity, maybe this was the place, and maybe this was where she was meant to go. When she arrived she had no idea what to expect. The ceilings were so high it strained her neck to look up, and everything was a steely white. The nuns reminded her of penguins, nodding their heads at the slightest provocation and trying to look pleasant and agreeable all the time as if they had been born with a smile.

Peck. Peck. Peck. The nun's pasted smiles leapt at her. She flinched. She was in a nunland.

After her mother left, one of the more severe looking nuns ushered her into a dormitory with several other girls, all gleaming and smiley in their white, perfectly ironed *shalwar kameezs*. She sat on what they told her was her bed for a while, and then suddenly she started feeling choked with fear and a deep sense of loss.

How she longed to be held by her mother. However angry she was with her mother, there was nothing like her baby memories of being in her arms, safe and comfortable, warmed by the soft folds of her skin, breathing her air, away from the prying eyes of this new and frightening world. Peck peck peck. The next morning the nuns marched into their rooms, ordering them to go to the bathroom and wash up. Zaib tried not to stand too close to the other girls as they waited their turns. After they had all had baths, they were faced with mashed potatoes and what looked like the rubber eggs that Zaib used to feed Barbie at home.

In the first few days no one spoke to her, in fact most of the students avoided her. At meal times they looked at her from the corner of their eye suspiciously. At night when she couldn't sleep she bit back the tears and counted backwards from one to a hundred to try and get to sleep. It usually took at least an hour, but sleep was welcome when it came because at least it meant she could escape to her dreams.

A week later, a Hindu girl, Pretima, who was also relatively new at the convent, approached her. They struck up a conversation and in time they became close enough to discuss everyday issues, classes and sometimes even their plans for the future. A few more weeks passed and Zaib felt she was finally settling in. She had a feeling that the girls knew her religious background, she thought she had heard snippets here and there that suggested they did.

But one day she was confronted by it head on. She had just finished her Maths class and was walking down a long grey corridor to the next one when Saira, one of the girls in her class, came and stood in front of her blocking her way.

'Hey Zaib. I know whose daughter you are.'

'So?' she said defiantly.

'So I know that you father is a Muslim and your mother a Christian.'

Zaib felt faint. Fear has many faces, but the fear she felt now, she knew well because it was the same fear she had felt in her old school, walking down her old street and in her worst nightmares. Inside she prayed, please God please not again, please let her go away – somehow. She said nothing, but the girl went on, 'So what do you believe in, Christianity or Islam?'

She heard herself say, 'I believe in both.'

The girl looked horrified, 'You can't believe in BOTH,' she said shocked.

The next day the news had spread and the disgusted looks Zaib received from other girls was a familiar one. She stayed as close to Pretima as possible as a refuge from them. Pretima told her to ignore them as everyone else had always told her to. 'They tell me I pray to statues because I am Hindu and I have learnt to ignore it.'

'*But I can't.* If only it was that simple.'

And Zaib was an *untouchable* once again. There must be something wrong with me *inside*, she thought. Zaib was at the convent for three years. Other than Pretima she made no new friends. Pretima was kind and caring, but something was missing, a sort of passion, warmth she craved. What she did find in Pretima instead was a dependable friend, someone who could be relied upon and would give sound advice when needed. She was someone who stood by her, strangely without the emotion.

The rest of her time was spent reading and studying. She started to excel in her studies, especially in Chemistry and Biology and in time she decided that she wanted to be a doctor like her mother. When she told mummy, she was elated, but because the best pre-medical college was in Lahore, she had to leave the convent the following year. This time she was going to be stronger, she promised herself that she wouldn't let anyone get away with abusing her or her family. Being away from her family at the convent had given her armour; it had made her more resilient, more equipped to deal with the world.

I have seen love in your eyes – I have seen a tear...

ঙ৪ঌ

5

Ghazala

Alya knew too well that Zaib had always been highly imaginative, consumed by thoughts of matchstickmen, fairies, elves, gnomes and other fantastical creatures venturing into many mysterious and mystical unknown worlds. The matchstickmen were the *outsiders*. She told Alya once, 'When I told mummy and daddy about the matchstickmen they looked terrified, as if something horrible had happened to me. It frightened me. That night there were upside down pictures in my head and I flew like mad, trying to free myself. In the morning I woke up to Ralph rocking backwards and forwards laughing insanely.'

Oh yes, thought Alya, the all-too-familiar matchstickmen were always there, cutting us up at will, recreating our thoughts and actions for us, re-inventing our lives and throwing us away just as easily. We dissolve and then we are reborn as something else or something altered. After all Zaib was right when she said that she was just trying to be herself. But the difference between most of us is that we have hardened to the matchstickmen, we have learnt to survive them, even believe them at times. That is our weakness. But not Zaib, she tried to live outside them, she wanted to expel them from her life and it had cost her.

From what she had told Alya, in Zaib's darkest times Ralph seemed to be her only saviour. Zaib had described Ralph to Alya in great detail, with his pointed nose and large black eyes, his olive shoes and his blistering outbursts when he was angry. 'The "grown-ups" never saw him, but he was there.' He anchored her when she needed someone the most, sobbing into her pillow or simply questioning the order of things she couldn't understand. During dark and lonely evenings when her mother was playing bridge with friends or when she could hear the incessant chatter of her parents' guests, she would sit and talk to Ralph for hours. And he helped her survive the grueling comments and accusations of her aunts, who visited the house frequently. Ruksana Khala was particularly spiteful and she related several stories about her to Alya from time to time. She would, for example, make it a point to comment on Zaib's looks whenever she visited. Once she told her, '*Beta* you look so thin and dark. What is wrong with you, have some milk, brighten up that face otherwise you will remain a spinster all your life.'

At another time she told Zaib's mother, 'Zaib's nose has definitely gone on her father's side of the family.'

She knew what that meant. For several days after that Zaib kept pinching her nose and staring at it in the mirror, thinking of ways to make it thinner.

These were just a few of the comments she was subjected to month after month. Zaib felt increasingly isolated and desolate. Slowly she was slipping into herself, looking for a place to hide and be safe, away from her khalas, her mother, her life as it was, with her father as her only ally.

Her mother was working at a government hospital on the Mall (the Ganga Ram Hospital) where Zaib recalled the road always smelt of methylated spirit and the street corners were littered with dirty towels and blood-stained bits of cotton wool. There was a butcher's shop just opposite the hospital, and Zaib frequently saw cats eating scraps of meat and skin on the footpath when she went to drop her mother to the hospital. White meat. Dead meat. A syringe fear in her gut. The drive to the hospital had left her with horror in her head. At home, in the evenings, her mother would discuss her patients with her father, while Zaib listened with fascination as a silent spectator, barely noticed by her mother. Her father listened intently moving his toes in a circle and then up and down finally stretching them as far as he could.

Then came Ghazala, unexpectedly, as if from the trees. At the time Zaib met Ghazala she was thirteen. Zaib would always refer to her as her *soulmate*. 'She was my first love,' she told Hassan once. The two girls first saw each other in Zaib's golden garden. For Zaib her garden was her refuge, her shelter, a vast wonderland of fantasies with its huge lush green mango trees and rain-coloured rose gardens. It was her haven. One evening when Zaib looked up she saw that the shredded sky had spread pink veins across the horizon and she felt she could almost smudge the colours with her small fingers; it reminded her of strawberry and vanilla ice-cream all mixed up. All she had to do was hold it all in her head. It was about to rain. She opened her palms and raised them towards the sky. Gradually, red mirages in the sky began to dissolve and the sky became overcast with grey clouds.

Zaib looked at her doll, Sonia, lying limply in her lap. Sonia had blue-green glass eyes and a permanent smile and her inability to move suddenly unnerved Zaib as did the thought of an impending downpour that would interfere with her plan of playing in the garden that evening. The cry came to her out of the black sky without warning. It was the cry of a child. It felt far away, yet it was clearer than rain and she was curious to find out where it was coming from. A purple sky cast a shadow on the steps of the veranda and she could hear the pitter patter of tiny frogs feet on the ground. As the cries became louder, she began to walk towards the sound. It was coming from the servant's quarter where the gardener and his family lived right at the far end of the garden behind the house.

Zaib had never thought about the gardener having a family and though she knew where the servant's quarter was, she had been strictly forbidden by her mother to visit it, who told her, 'I never want to see you near the servant's quarter. These people carry all sorts of germs on their clothes and some of them even have lice in their hair, *acha*? I don't want you to get ill *beta*.'

Despite her mother's warnings Zaib didn't understand the difference. She had grown up with beggars on the streets all around her and though she, like the millions of others frequenting the streets of Pakistan, were largely anesthetized by their presence and their perseverance for a few rupees, she still felt sorry for them and wished she could help them in some way. She knew her mother felt sorry for them too, but that did not mean she considered them her *equal*.

While trying to get to the child she recalled fondly the many occasions, she had sat on the gardener's lap and played with his hair by emptying talcum powder on it and rubbing it into his scalp, he would bend his head down obediently to go through the same procedure again and again, while Zaib would giggle uncontrollably. She wondered how many children he had and who the crying child was. He was too old to have a child that age, it must be a grandchild, she thought. She found out a few days later that he was Ghazala's stepfather and the child was Ghazala's baby sister.

She finally arrived at the servants' quarter and crept up to the jagged planks of wood nailed together that were the door.

A whiff of my sweet love, swept through me... and the nude room.

The once white paint, now moon yellow had peeled off the walls almost completely. She opened the door slowly, nervously. She automatically took off her *chappals* and stepped onto an uneven floor almost too hot for her to stand on. Ants had made their home in the cracks on the wall, disappearing and re-appearing in seconds, some balancing a new load of food to take home, others just busily passing by as if this were just a stop over on a long journey. A still heat hung in the middle of the room. The ants pinned her down until she looked up again and saw her.

A girl dressed in a purple *shalwar kameez,* a little older than her, knelt on the ground to lift something from the floor. Next to her a child of about two sat wailing continuously. Her face was covered with tears and smut and every time she rubbed her face with her hands it became grayer and dirtier. Zaib could hear more screams and crying coming from further inside. She imagined there was also an older woman probably cooking at a stove in another room, like she had seen in Hindi movies. The girl in front of her looked prematurely old by the faint lines circling her mouth and the ironic expression in her eyes, yet when she did eventually look up, she seemed to smile a little. It was the smile of a child on a woman's face. By this time the girl was squatting on the floor, trying to pacify the wailing child by picking her by carelessly and shaking her vigorously – an act she had obviously performed many times before – as if she were a rag doll. She then slapped the child on its back several times, but the child was relentless. She looked up as if by chance and saw a girl about her age in a red dress staring at her. She looked at her questioningly but there was no explanation from Zaib, who was suddenly lost for words. The girl, whose name she later learned was Ghazala, was visibly irritated and annoyed at being disturbed.

Zaib found her voice at last, 'Are you the gardener's daughter?'

'Who are you?' she asked accusingly.

'This is my house.'

'My father says we are not supposed to call you in here or talk to you but you can have some tea if you like.'

'Can I have a Pepsi?'

The girl looked uncomfortable and even though Zaib was a child herself she realized her mistake.

'I've changed my mind, yes tea please.'

Ghazala picked up the baby's feeding bottle of what was obviously milk, but what from the consistency of it looked more like water with white paint in it. She shoved the nipple in the child's mouth roughly and within a minute or so the baby went to sleep in Ghazala's lap. She lifted the baby and casually put it on a *charpoy* that was lying on one side of the room and covered the child with her *dupatta*. Then she went into another room for a few minutes, while Zaib sat next to the baby waiting and wondering what she should do or say next when the girl came back.

There was a musty smell of dust in the room and a few small white pieces of cloth made out of *mal mal,* soiled with the baby's urine lay next to the bed. The walls had large watermarks on them from where the rain had seeped into them and the ceiling fan, which seemed unstable by the way it wobbled unnervingly while it rotated round and round, had wires protruding from its base, giving Zaib the uneasy feeling that it might fall on her at any moment.

Spiders in ecstasy whisper their last.

Ghazala interrupted her thoughts when she came back with tea. The cups were chipped at the edges and the saucers had brown stains on them. Zaib hesitated for a moment before taking the cup from her, but then gently took it and started drinking. They finished their tea without a word. After they had finished Zaib said she had to go as her mother may be looking for her and left.

That night she felt a strange emptiness inside that she hadn't encountered before and for a long time she lay in bed thinking of the strange girl she had met that day. They didn't meet again until three days later when the milk boy rang the doorbell to deliver milk one morning and Zaib ran to answer it. Ghazala was washing clothes just in front of her quarter, under a running tap. She was squatting on the floor, rubbing a bright yellow soap bar onto a piece of cloth vigorously with one hand and holding down the cloth with the other. When she saw Zaib looking at her, she spoke first.

'Do you want to me to put mehndi on your palms tonight, Zaib baaji? I can do it for you.'

That evening Zaib sneaked out of the house when mummy and daddy were with guests in the lounge or as Zaib always called it, the *crystal room.*

Ghazala had prepared the thick green-brown paste and was swirling a matchstick in it when Zaib walked in that evening. She sat down on the *charpoy* and Ghazala started making intricate designs on her palms. It was like magic, Zaib imagined it was an old Moorish design sculpted on a castle wall and they were both princesses adorning each other. She filled her palms with curious designs and finished off the last of them with a look of satisfaction. Zaib told her that her parents would be out that evening and that they could meet again. So it was settled and that night they spent hours in the garden sitting next to a huge willow tree talking about the great spirits, *the jinns* that often live under old trees.

'I know a *jinn* that lives here, but he is not a bad *jinn,* he is good and kind and we can feast with him whenever we want.'

Zaib could barely contain her wonder as she travelled with Ghazala to distant lands of the most enchanting sights and sounds created by the good *jinns.*

Over the next few weeks the two girls became inseparable. Somehow she seemed wise and far beyond her years, she was the most curious creature Zaib had ever seen, like a willow, mournful and serene, a mountain that's seen a thousand civilizations and yet remains as fresh and new as the brightest star in the sky on a black night. They had a deep understanding of each other's thoughts and every time they left each other they couldn't wait to be together again. There were times when Zaib wanted to take Ghazala into her arms and disappear, so that nobody could find them, so that neither of them could ever be separated or have to hide from prying eyes. Sometimes Zaib talked to sparrows to help them escape. Sometimes she clasped her hands and prayed like Devika, her sister, kneeling in front of God but not to escape from her troubles or to ask for anything more, but simply for God never to take away what she had. She held Ghazala's hands and plucked diamonds out of the sky and for now she was safe with Ghazala: the *matchstickmen* were worlds away. With Ghazala by her side Zaib at last felt secure and content. At night she longed to be held by her and she had an ache in the pit of her stomach in her yearning for her. They listened to the sound of a common pulse for hours and taught themselves how to hear words forming in the wind so that people couldn't munch them before they were said. It mattered less to Zaib what the *matchstickmen* thought of love or what people said between laughs and prayers when Ghazala was with her.

There is a quietness in my love's arms that makes me want to go back to before mummy and daddy (when I am born I will count backwards if I can't sleep at night, like I used to in my last hours of quiet).

One weekend Zaib's parents were visiting relatives in Faisalabad and she was left to the care of Tara, her maid and the family cook, Badar. It was the time of the biggest annual religious ceremony in the old city of Lahore, where Zaib's ancestors were born and where many of their houses still stood in ruins. It was a yearly ritual, celebrating the death anniversary of Munir Shah, a saint who had died more than five hundred years ago. Zaib had only been to the old city a couple of times with her parents, to participate in the spring festival of *basanth* where she had seen people slicing the flat sky with kites, a festival that had seemed particularly pointless to her and one that she had seen no reason to be a part of again.

Ghazala told her that it was the custom for her and her family to pray at the tomb of the saint every year. This year she wanted Zaib to join her in her prayers. She said that if Zaib prayed at his tomb, she would be given anything she asked for. Until now Zaib hadn't associated the old city with death or ghosts. After listening to how revered the saint was, Zaib imagined his hair still growing out of his head. (She had heard her mother telling someone hair and nails continue to grow for a while even after death). The saint became a powerful soothsayer in his grave with nails as long as trees winding their way through the roots of plants and hair slicing the heads off worms busy with their food and families. She stared at Ghazala with wide eyes.

'Zaib you don't understand, this way God will never separate us.'

God can't do that. *God can do anything.*

Zaib had to convince her maid who was also a religious woman. 'Tara, God will be so happy with me and I promise to be back by 10 pm.' Tara agreed but only if she could join them too. Zaib agreed reluctantly but told her not to tell her mother that she and Ghazala were friends. It was six in the evening; Ghazala wrapped a *dupatta* around Zaib's head tightly so that her hair would be hidden. The ritual had begun at home.

'You look beautiful.'

Zaib peered at herself in the mirror in wonder at how different she looked, and yes she was right, at how beautiful she looked.

They left in a group, Zaib, Ghazala, Tara and her cousins, most of them male. Women were advised not to go on their own in case they were harassed or stalked. They walked to the end of the street Zaib lived on and turned a corner where there were at least fifty people waiting to catch the next wagon that was to take them to the old city. Most of the women were in *burkas,* their lips and noses hidden. Zaib looked up at them in awe. For her they were nymphs, with shimmering black cloaks billowing in the night like waves in the sea when the moon was hidden by clouds. Their proud eyes punctured the noise of traffic outside Zaib hated so much and she felt at peace. She clutched Ghazala's *dupatta* and savoured the air. A halo of lamplight surrounded her as she and the crowd around her stood in unison waiting to reach a common destination. She reached out every now and again to catch a bit of lamplight in her small hands and for an instant she felt as if she were in heaven surrounded by angels that were there to protect her.

'Will there be a lot of men with beards and caps on?' The excitement in her was rising. But as soon as she had said it, she was glad Ghazala didn't hear her.

The wagon arrived and all fifty people fought to climb on at once. It creaked as it stood there gyrating from one side to another while one passenger after another fought to climb on. They pushed and elbowed their way through the crowd trying to get inside the door, and after a final struggle, the first to get inside sat down on the seats, others climbed onto the roof and held on to the railings. It was a desperate race and Zaib just stood staring until she felt Ghazala push her ahead of her and force her to sit down on a seat while she stood next to her leaning on the back of her seat. Zaib tried not to hold on to Ghazala as the car skidded at almost every turn. The wagon sounded like a thousand pieces of metal rattling against the windows and Zaib closed her eyes tightly to shut out the noise.

By the time they reached Zaib's bones were aching and she felt sick and dizzy. She stepped outside, still slightly disorientated.

The street was almost brighter than day with artificial light. Bent trees lining either side of the road sparkled with hundreds of tiny multi-coloured light bulbs. A procession of people streamed the roads, blocking all traffic. The sides of the roads were dotted with stalls selling a variety of items. Children cried, the reflection of coloured lights in their eyes, and sulked when they couldn't buy something they wanted; one rubbed her face in her mother's breasts while pulling her hair. Her mother looked fed up and tired as if she was ready to throw the child away. Street vendors had set up several small markets selling bangles, cloth, imitation jewellery, old clothes, cassettes, and most intriguingly for Zaib florescent plastic snakes and lizards which she kept in her head for the rest of the night as a weapon against Ruksana Khala.

Salesmen shouted to each other across stalls, exchanging goods, giving orders to the next person and cursing the demanding customer. Ghazala bought a Michael Jackson T-shirt for her brother and Zaib bought red and green glass bangles for herself.

It was dinnertime and Zaib was starving. She could almost taste it, so strong was the aroma of food in the air. Smoke tails from food being cooked on mobile cookers behind the stalls, rose and disappeared into thin air, tapering into the sky, serpents sinking into oblivion, wiped out in seconds. At every step there were food stalls selling either *jalebis*, other varieties of *mithai* and different curries. She told Ghazala she was hungry and one of Ghazala's male cousins bought them a plate of food. It was a thick sauce with chickpeas and a chapatti soaked in it. Zaib could see a dead mosquito lying sprawled in the curry and felt sick. When she pointed it out to Ghazala, she smiled dismissively, picked it up with her fingers and flicked it away. After they'd all eaten they walked on for another hour. Zaib felt like a bird. She floated through the crowd in a state of somnambulism. By now she was convinced God was walking with her.

Many streets later, they reached the tomb where the birth of the dead saint was being celebrated. Zaib had never felt her heart beat so fast. She clung to Ghazala and at the same time tried not to blink in case she missed something as her eyes widened.

In the middle of the crowd there was a tombstone on a raised platform covered with a black velvet cloth, intricately embroidered with gold thread. Covering half of it was a white sheet with stains of crushed red roses on it faintly visible through the blanket of garlands that covered it, some rose, others jasmine and *raat ki raani*. The rich smell of roses edged black streaked the wind. Women and men circled the tomb slowly, one by one, pursing their lips with their eyes shut lightly and their hands raised, praying to the saint, their hopes pinned on a man long gone. An old woman with matted hair and rags for clothes sat on one side of the tombstone with her face covering her hands, rocking backwards and forwards mumbling some verses loudly. On the other side sat a group of men in torn clothes and knotted disheveled hair playing the *tabla*, swaying from side to side to the sound of the drum beat; mops of knotted dust caked hair slapped their faces and shoulders. Dressed in black they shared the death dance in a drugged frenzy. They rolled their eyes, so that only the cornea was visible, eyelids fluttering in front of the bulbous white mass like butterflies in ecstasy. Their sweat splattering the air as there bodies shook uncontrollably. The smoky smell (that Zaib later learnt was of marijuana) rose causing a white film across the dark sky and made her feel lightheaded and nostalgic. In one corner a thin man with a white beard and deep lines on his forehead and cheeks that looked as if they had been penciled on his face, sat, cross-legged munching a paan, hurling abuses at the musicians. He had one white eye and broken brown teeth. Every now and then he spat out a thick brown liquid caught by the hungry air of human hums and pains. A few moments later Zaib saw two men in uniforms beating him with sticks and dragging him across the floor. She heard them call him the son of Satan.

The experience of that night left its remnants in bits and pieces of dreams to come, transforming the world into a mystical place, it left its reflection in books and conversations Zaib had with others, in long nights of lovemaking with Hassan and in her quiet sobs in bed when the children had gone to sleep. Zaib often tried to recall the finer details of the night that seemed to stretch beyond time, as if something had been left unfinished. The men and the women had offered their devotion and their children had struggled to get away. Ghazala had prayed and made a wish, stone still, with head slightly tilted upwards towards God and her hands cupped in front of her, waiting for the answer to gently drop into her hungry hands. Was it water through a fisherman's net? Did her prayers ever get answered? She had wondered what Ghazala was praying for but she dared not ask. On the way back the familiar sound of the *azaan* filled her heart and her mind with joy. In that voice was hope, love, beauty, peace, all wrapped into one. It was about a year after that that Zaib started to think deeply about the pattern of Ghazala's thoughts on that day and she wished so much she had asked her. She wished she had. When she came home that night she slept with Ghazala in her room, with her arms tightly locked around her, absorbed by her.

Several days later after Zaib's parents were back from their visit to Faisalabad, her mother caught her in the servant's quarter with Ghazala playing Ludo. This was not the first time she had caught them together. She told Zaib it was highly inappropriate.

'If you don't stop meeting this girl, these people will be asked to leave!'

The ultimatum had been given and Zaib felt as if someone was choking her. She cried herself to sleep for several days after that and hardly spoke to her mother or her father. She couldn't understand why it was so difficult for her mother to let her be happy for a change. But she also knew that if she disobeyed her she would have to bear the loss of seeing Ghazala leave, so she decided to tell Ghazala the truth.

'Ghazala, my mother has told me not to visit you anymore. What do we do now?'

Ghazala smiled, almost as if she had half expected it. 'It's ok, Zaib. You won't understand but we are used to this. We will meet when they are busy or out and I can still come and see you when you are playing outside. Just don't come to the quarter when they are home and keep singing our songs, that way you'll be with me and I'll be thinking of you.'

That worked out well for them for some time and they managed to meet almost as often as before as Zaib's parents remained busy during most of the day.

But then came the summer. The dreaded summer and Nathia Gali. That's when they all went to their annual trip to Nathia Gali, in the north of Pakistan, for a holiday. Usually Zaib looked forward to the trip, but this year it meant being away from Ghazala for more than two months and she could hardly bear to even think of such a long separation. She begged her parents not to go, but once again her mother threatened to 'get rid' of Ghazala if she persisted.

Her mother was shaking her, 'Stop throwing a tantrum. I know exactly why you want to stay Zaib and it's not acceptable!'

After that Zaib didn't complain. She went with them quietly, but she refused to eat properly and spent the next few months dreaming about what she could have been doing if she were with Ghazala. She also had time to think of all the things she and Ghazala had talked including the things she still wanted to talk to her about. Strangely, she had never asked Ghazala anything about her family or about who lived in the servant's quarter apart from her and her father, the gardener. There was so much she still wanted to know about Ghazala's life. Yet, it was as if they shared the same blood, the same brain, pulse, hands, and thoughts. It was as if they were the same being and although she had no contact with her during those two months, she had their songs as Ghazala had said.

Finally, after two interminable months without her, it was time to go home. Zaib could barely contain her happiness. She had managed to buy Ghazala a garland of *raat ki rani*, her favourite flower and she had collected colourful semi-precious stones for her that she knew would fascinate her. They finally arrived and Zaib ran to the servant's quarters immediately. Her heart beat furiously and her stomach ached. She banged on the door. *A whiff of her and me and the nude room.*

'Ghazala, open, I'm back!'

When she looked down, she noticed the door was padlocked.

'Mummy, mummy!!! Mama where are they?'

'Honey I have to speak to you.' It was something about the way her mother said it. She sensed something terrible was going to happen.

'Zaib let's go inside, darling, there is something I have to tell you. Sweetheart I thought it best to tell you when we got home. I got a message from Badar a few days ago.'

Zaib was staring at her with a glazed expression in her eyes. Mother held her hands.

'My angel, Ghazala is …'

She could barely make out the words.

Mother was a butcher.

I am not an angel.

She and I have lived a long time now in the grass, which looks at me from between the sharp white tingling rays, smiling in the winter and couched warmly in the hours of my choice – hidden, where closets save old specks of dust far from the resounding chatter of crickets outside. She disturbs me; my love, now gone so far… but so does this ice-cream cone in my hand, so full of coldness and sugar, telling me my teeth will rot with microscopic organisms I will never see, burrowing their under-nourished protrusions into my teeth. It is just right now, at this moment, when the summer is rife with flies screening the tips of my fingers and the flowers on her grave, their greedy heads moving sharply from side to side, that I realize my teeth are unique and will, one day, save my soul in the ground of its choosing and that the cone and I have nothing to worry about. Perhaps she doesn't either… anymore.

☙❧

6

Hassan

Zaib stirred. Alya knew it was going to be difficult but it had to be done. Zaib was slipping again. Strings. Strings. Strings. Get the strings together.

The first thing to do was to call the doctor, get him to come over as soon as possible. She wished her father was there. Where are you today, so kind and so strong, capable of taking care of things? Her father, whom she had admired and looked up to, her rock, the man whom she thought was invincible. They had all been singed by what had happened. Blame, guilt, anger, fear; they were all part of a process that each one of them went through. They had all lived through their personal hell, and though that time had gone its remains had lingered, in their thoughts, their actions, their words, their gestures and those small things that were left unsaid between them.

Nothing is ever lost, the air around you picks up your moans, your aches and delivers them to you on a platter when you least expect it. Everything unfolds in its own unique way catching you off guard at the most unexpected moments. Is that why I feel so desolate in this dark place I call home, thought Alya, cradled only by the wind and the little trinkets I have collected from the past to keep me standing. I live surrounded by a self-constructed world, whispering half-truths to myself. In the end the only thing that is of value is the spirit of the thing that once was. Its like love, its essence, its everlasting bitter sweetness is with us, if it wasn't we would not survive; it is the sole reason we live.

Had it not been for love the earth would be an empty, barren place. And yet ironically it is always love that kills you in the end. Wasn't it love that had bound her parents in that inexplicable devotion that took them to the boundaries of hell and back? Hassan and Zaib, the couple that they all said defined love. Was that possible, ever? Ammi said it was. Ammi *knew* it was.

'When Zaib first met Hassan, she was only a child,' Devi khala had told her. 'She was barely fourteen, but I knew from the look in her eyes that he would be the one.'

Alya had such a clear picture of how they met that it was almost as if she was there. The stories had been told to her by different sources over and over again and of course Zaib had never ceased to furnish her daughters' knowledge with how much she had loved their father and of the various *journeys* they went on and how much he adored her.

'He was my Oberon, you know, and I his Titania. We always loved each other in every way possible and he knew everything, always.'

They first met at a park. She had been perched on a tree swinging her legs backwards and forwards, when the branch cracked and she panicked and jumped. The height of the fall wasn't great, until she looked up and saw a young man, of about eighteen standing in front of her. She smiled sheepishly as he helped her up. Hassan was the son of Riffat and Junaid, close friends of her parents, but she had never met him before. Over the next few months, as the families seemed to get closer, he and his parents started to visit more often. Zaib was drawn to his kind demeanor that told her she had nothing to worry about if he was with her. They struck up a friendship quickly and she waited for his visits anxiously.

By the time she was sixteen, Zaib knew there was something more to their relationship. Devi once told Alya it was like he was an intrinsic part of her. Hassan was, by nature, loving and protective and he found in her a childlike quality that was rare. She fascinated him with her imaginative stories and her curiosity about the world and its creatures. He hadn't met any one with such a strong love of life, such a passion for the simplest things that others took for granted. He savoured her love, her little attachments, but he also felt her sensitivity, from the first day they had met, he knew she was tender, someone who had to be handled with care and understanding and he promised himself he would be the one to look after her.

Zaib had prided herself on the way she always took care of her father's needs, but in the end somewhere inside her, she felt she had betrayed him for Hassan. That had irked her throughout her years with Hassan, yet Hassan was her love, the man she was meant to be with, she was sure of that. In Zaib's mind there was a pattern and a reason for the way things turned out just like her father had said, then why didn't he understand? He had said, 'Beta, you are still young and I have seen the world change a million times. I know you think you love him but he is not the man for you.'

She clearly recalled the hue of that day. Lollipop trees sprouted red, purple, and yellow. It was April and the city was streaked with colour. Her mother was hanging out the clothes to dry because the maid was ill and had not come in to work. Mother looked particularly gentle and Zaib had a sudden urge to hug her, remove the wrinkle from the corner of her mouth, and tell her how much she loved her, but somehow she just couldn't do it. Instead she just smiled at her and hoped she would understand what lay behind her smile. If mother noticed, Zaib didn't know about it.

At dinner her father was not there. He had been missing meals with the family with increasing frequency. Initially, Zaib thought he was working on a difficult case, but after some time she became concerned.

'Mummy, why isn't daddy coming to dinner these days?'

'He's not too well Zaib.'

'Why didn't you tell me? What's wrong?'

'Why don't you go and see him after dinner Zaib and you can talk to him yourself.'

After dinner she knocked on the door.

'Come in Zaib.'

His dark form shifted from one corner of the room to another. He held a book in his hand and waved it in the air.

'It's been some time my little angel. Come here, sit next to me.... so the young people of today don't need their old parents any more, ha?' He chuckled. As she got closer his silhouette melted into an old, frail looking man.

He spelt out her guilt and she felt uncomfortable. She was scared to get too close. He sat back from her as if he had sensed her apprehension.

'So let's first get to the most important issue at hand, that of this young man Hassan. How serious is it?'

'I love him.'

'He is a good man, but Zaib I don't think he is for you. You need something more.'

'Daddy, I know he is the one and I know he will look after me.'

'But will he give you what you need. You are so full of wonder, my child. *Beta*, you are larger than life. You need a man your equal.'

Her equal? What was that supposed to mean? Daddy had a habit of trying to make her feel better than the rest as if she was superior in some way and sometimes it made her feel important, but now, usually it just made her angry. She just wanted him to approve that's all. It was that simple. For the first time in her life she felt bitterness towards him.

He paused and then continued, 'I could go on, but I can see that I am not going to be able to convince you, but remember once you are married you have to try and make it work, it is a commitment. You must learn to love and care for each other.'

'I will daddy. You don't think he's that bad, do you?'

'No I don't think he's that bad. I just want the best for my baby that's all.'

'Maybe he is the best for me daddy.'

'Yes, maybe he is.'

'Daddy, please trust me.'

'I do Zaib. You will and must do what your heart wills you to do, you have my opinion, and if you try hard enough it will work. Come here, a bit closer, I want to talk to you about something.'

She put her hand on her father's. She could feel the contours of his veins underneath her fingers and she felt comforted and secure.

'Zaib you are going to start a new life soon and you will see many many years of joy and you will experience great love in your life with your own children and your husband. Beta, I don't want to hide anything from you. There is a lot of happiness ahead of you. I went to the doctor recently; he told me I have cancer. Now listen,' he clutched her hand tightly, 'don't tell your sister just yet. She has just got married and we still have time so you have to promise not to tell her just yet. I am sorry Zaib.'

Before she could understand, before the pictures came into her head the word fell from her lips listlessly, 'Promise.'

And that was it... like drawing a line on a blank page. She felt her hands go numb and the feeling in her legs died. She slowly lifted her hand from his and looked at him accusingly. Her throat was dry and she felt her chest constrict.

'You can't do this to me.'

'Zaib, no one is here forever and it would be torture if one was, I would be miserable. I have lived my life, I have had many wonderful moments with you and with your mother, with your brothers and sisters and now I am ready to go. You must live on and have your own children and they their own and the cycle goes on.'

The thought of life without him was unimaginable. Her chest tightened. For a long time she sat with her hand lying limply next to his, what would it be like after he'd gone? What would she do now? Who would tell her what was right, what was wrong, how to look at the world and see the wonder in the tiniest of God's creations. She left his room in a daze. The last look she saw in his eyes before she left him was one of guilt. He looked almost apologetic for dying.

Initially she couldn't bear to spend too much time with him.

A week went by. It was late at night.

'Zaib, why aren't you seeing your father these days?'

'I'm busy with college mummy.'

'Zaib, I know it's difficult but for now we all have to put our feelings aside and think of him first, he needs us. We can't just abandon him.'

'But he is leaving me forever mummy!' She sobbed into her mother's chest.

'Zaib, I love him too, but he is ill, it's not his fault.'

It crossed her mind that he was dying because of mummy, but then she saw the tenderness in her mother's eyes, in her hands, her words, in everything she did for daddy in his last days. Had she never seen that before or had she simply ignored the good things and focused on the bad ones? Were there things she didn't know about them? Were they secretly, deeply in love?

How strange mummy was. All these years she had fought with him over the smallest things, yet she always managed to pull through when he had needed her most. She recalled a few years earlier when he had contracted typhoid, she was at his bedside day and night. She had hardly eaten in those few weeks when he was at his worst. Her dedication as his wife, his companion was unequalled and yet she could be so cruel to him. Zaib had watched her and thought to herself at the time that

that kind of caring and could only have come from love and yet why couldn't she see it all those years when she was growing up and how could mummy be so terrible to someone she loved so much? And then it dawned on her. She saw that it could take seconds to discount two people's love for each other, and brand them enemies, yet it can take a lifetime to understand their 'love'.

With time, Zaib resumed her old conversations with daddy, they argued about the same old things. They wandered in the garden on days he felt strong enough to take a walk with her. As the days wore on, she hoped the cancer would go away. Soon the chemotherapy began and her father's beautiful silver hair was gone. His eyes looked hollow and his cheeks were grey. Zaib was crippled.

She overheard him talking to her mother in the bedroom one evening.

'I can't do this anymore. I am too old now. Just tell them to stop. Please.'

'We have to try. You could live for years. Just a few more months and then there will be a break. Don't argue with me on this. I won't let you be so defeatist about this. You have to be strong.'

That was so like her, thought Zaib.

'Please, just let me go in peace.'

There was a flat silence after that while Zaib anxiously waited for a response.

The next day when father came back from the hospital he was smiling.

'I feel so fresh today. They told me that I don't need to go for my treatment anymore. I am better.'

She saw the lie in his eyes.

But on this one she didn't fight him. It was time for her to give him back what he had given her since the day she was born.

'Yes daddy, you look better.'

She and her mother exchanged glances.

Zaib and daddy took their meals together, they exchanged notes on books they'd read and talked about his past and Zaib's favourite topics of discussion. But this time it wasn't her mother she wanted to talk about, it was Fatima, his first wife, whom she asked about incessantly.

'Why did you divorce her daddy? Didn't you love her?'

He explained that in *those days* the family arranged marriages and you didn't have much choice about whom you married. The same was the case with him and Fatima. She was his first cousin and both sets of parents had agreed that when Shafi turned eighteen they would get them married. Fatima was ten years older than him, which he explained, was also not uncommon in those days. She was pleasant in her demeanour and trained as a perfect housewife by her mother; she was excellent at cooking and cleaning and looking after the children. He told her the routine and each aspect of his past life in detail as if he wanted his daughter to have the satisfaction of keeping every part of his story after he was gone. He said that every morning before going to work his shoes were shining. His breakfast was ready and his clothes were hanging at the exact same place everyday, flawlessly ironed. When he came home, dinner was on the table at the stroke of eight and their four children were placed at their respective seats like little dolls.

One day he asked Fatima in a genuinely curious manner, 'Fatima, why isn't anything ever dirty or out of place in this house?'

'What? Don't you like it this way? Am I doing something wrong?' She looked worried and confused.

'No, that's the problem. Look. I have an idea; let's go on holiday together, just the two of us? Let's leave all this pristine cleanliness and order and just go away.'

'What about the children?'

'They are old enough to stay on their own. Besides, we have the rest of the family to look after them.'

'We can't leave the children alone.'

'Fatima, our entire family is here, the children can stay with them.'

But Fatima was not convinced. She couldn't imagine leaving her home and going away, how would it run properly without her? And what would they do alone in a foreign place without the children? She told him he could go if he wanted to but that she had to stay and look after the children. The same was the case with business dinners and outings. She refused to accompany her husband as she said women are better off at home with the children. The outside world was a 'man's world'.

'You will be talking business. What place is that for women? I will be better off at home,' she would say.

When he invited his friends or colleagues home, she was awkward and uncomfortable.

'I know it sounds like a terrible thing to say Zaib, but she was not able to share my life with me the way I wanted her to and that affected our relationship.'

Even though Zaib had only seen her briefly once she felt a little sorry for her because she knew deep inside that it was she who had been left all alone when her father married her mother and that too with four children to look after. 'But you knew what she was like before you married her, so wasn't that unfair?'

'Well I was only eighteen, and knowing something and living through it are two entirely different things, you'll understand that one day. Maybe I was a little unfair, but I didn't know what it would be like actually living with her.'

Devi once told Zaib that she had heard Shafi didn't try hard enough with Fatima. 'She was full of vitality you know, she just didn't wear her heart on her sleeve like he did. He didn't give her a chance. He didn't try and find out.'

Zaib tried to imagine every aspect of their lives together. She wondered whose fault it really was. As he went on to explain it soon became obvious that they were two very different people who had nothing in common except their four children. When he eventually left her, Fatima lived through the shame of being a divorcee, a great taboo for a woman at the time and she was forced to give her family and friends explanations.

So it was her fault even though he was the one who had left her. First she had to face abandonment and then the cruelty of society. She told a friend, it was a shock when he said he wanted a divorce. 'I thought we were content.'

She nurtured her wounds quietly. After the emotional shock, there were practical concerns, how would she pay the bills, buy the groceries, look after herself and her children? The money wouldn't be a problem because she knew he wouldn't shirk his responsibilities, but it was just the dread of doing it all on her own. Life was so long. Then the shame, how would she handle the stigma? People would say she was a failed wife. And although she didn't show it, she hated him for doing that to her, for exposing her to the world and the taunts she would have to bear.

Their youngest daughter, Saima had told Devi, 'He was cursed by her, but had no idea and it was because he was so arrogant.'

When Fatima heard he had married a *Christian* woman only six months after their divorce, she knew she finally had her revenge. 'See, God heard me,' she told her sister, 'you can't get away with anything in this life.' The circle was complete and she had at last found some solace in his disgrace.

Zaib's mother had not allowed her daughters to meet their step sisters and brother and her father hadn't pressed the issue, but now more than ever she wanted to. She wanted to re-trace her father's steps.

'Daddy, I would love to meet my sisters and brothers once, it's been so many years.'

His eyes moistened, 'Nothing would make me happier.'

The ashtray stained with grey-black ash escapes the old cigar of daddy's mouth, a gaping urn echoing in his big empty room. Zaib, it's daddy, you are home now.

❧

Six months later her father died. Zaib slipped into shock. Her 'madness' manifested itself in her fascination with his trees and plants, the files he looked through so often in his room, the gas lamp he used to read under late at night when everyone was asleep. Zaib was often found talking to her father in the garden as if he were sitting between the branches of his trees, listening to every word carefully, lovingly. She became pale and sickly, a wanderer skirting the boundaries of his life, trying to understand its depths. Hassan tried to talk to her but she wouldn't let him in. Her mother tried but she shut her out too. She lived in a secluded state and refused to talk to anyone for more than three months. During that time she was heard talking to Ralph and Ghazala. They told her daddy was safe in heaven but heaven was here in his garden with him.

It took months before Zaib could understand that he was really gone. Looking at her mother lying so lifelessly in the bed next to her, Alya wondered how short the distance was between her mother and her grandfather. It wasn't long before Zaib would be back with her father, her present life a fragment of the past.

❧

The sun was bursting into Zaib's bedroom. She could see the milkman with his silver pot in his hand walking towards the house. He was always on time, like a machine. She wondered if he ever got fed up or bored. Mummy was putting away some clothes in her suitcase in the storeroom.

'Mummy what are you doing?'

She spoke in a small voice, which was not like her, 'I am just putting some things away that belonged to your father.'

'Mummy, are you alright?'

'Yes darling. I am fine. I just need some time on my own.'

'Should I call Devi?'

'No, no its ok, she needs to stay with her husband right now.'

Devi had visited once just before their father's death.

Mummy would stay in her room for hours. It worried Zaib to see the strongest person she knew suddenly look so weak and pale. She seemed to have aged decades in just a few months. Zaib felt so much closer to her in her vulnerability, but her mother had acquired a foreign look in her eyes, as if she was somewhere else, somewhere foreign where Zaib could not reach her.

The last thing she remembered her mother saying was, 'My place has and will remain with your father.' A few days later she had a heart attack and died. Within a year Zaib had lost both her parents. When Devika came back she refused to speak to her. She told her she wasn't there when she needed her. 'Where were you when he was dying? You are just so selfish Devi.' Devi said nothing but cried quietly in her room.

Zaib's last visit in that house was to her mother's storeroom, before packing up her things. She finally took out each piece of clothing and held it in front of her, clutching it tightly, crying because it had survived her mother. She would always associate the smell of mothballs with her parent's clothes, especially mummy's because her old wedding *joras* and college clothes were buried in big metal trunks with moth balls all around them so that the insects wouldn't eat them. Her clothes felt like water in her fingers, many of them untouched in suitcases for over half a century. Zaib held them tight and brought them close to her nose, inhaling deeply, inhaling the smell of her mother. Her blue and white school uniform still looked starched (she couldn't imagine mummy as a child). She missed her hands and her strange wisdom that so often perplexed her. She decided to take her mother's doilies with her to Zakar too. There were so many doilies, blue doilies, white doilies, pink doilies, faded doilies. The lace doilies were made around 1880 by mummy's mother so by now they were soft and delicate, almost crumbling in her hands. But Zaib loved them because of the fresh linen smell of 62E and because her mother was a part of them. Doilies, doilies, doilies!!! In doily land there were tea cups and warm tea and toast and honey and there was mother and daddy mixed up with all of that…

Zaib you will be taken away at 3 o' clock today.
Where will you put me?
On the red lily that floats in the ocean.
Why the red one?
Because it's your favourite, Zaib.
Do you see that little boy underneath that mango tree? He will show you. He is the baby you and Ghazala gave birth to. Zaib don't jump.
I can fly now.
Zaib, they won't save you.
Who?
The people with souls.
Do the matchstickmen have souls too?

Zaib was eventually left to the care of Hassan. Ruksana Khala with the other two khalas came to the house and wailed loudly to express their grief at the great tragedy that has befallen this 'once happy laughing family'. Zaib smiled ironically. After that day, she never met any of them again.

'Please take me away Hassan,' she told him. 'I don't want to come back here again.'

They left in silence taking only a few of her parent's belongings.

Hassan spoke to his parents about marrying Zaib. They had expected this but were hoping they would marry when Zaib was older. She was only eighteen. Hassan had just qualified as an architect and had applied for jobs in several countries including various Middle-Eastern countries. He felt there was little scope for him to succeed in Pakistan, besides he had always wanted to travel and work abroad.

While he waited for news, he and Zaib lived with his parents. She occasionally served tea to the family the way she imagined her mother would have taught her to. 'Zaib, you must look after your in-laws, they are after all your family after we are gone...' her mother had once told her. Even though they were at pains to make her feel at home, she sometimes resented them for being alive when her parents were dead, it just didn't seem fair. At other times she thought she caught Hassan's mother looking at her with pity and she hated that even more. When Zaib had her *nikaah* only family members were present, including Hassan's parents and their siblings and of course Devika. There was no festivity because Zaib's mother had not been dead a year and she was still supposed to be in mourning. But Zaib had also heard that Hassan's parents were trying to avoid the embarrassment of their son marrying into the Shafi family. 'How can they be so duplicitous?' She had asked Hassan. 'They were their friends?' She had heard that people had told Hassan a 'small affair' would be more appropriate for a girl who had lost both her parents in such quick succession. Zaib had dreamt of dressing up as a bride, even as a child and she resented being forced to make a show of her grief. How dare they make a mockery out of her parents' death by behaving as if they cared? She deliberately smiled as much as she could during the *nikaah*, shunning the hypocrisies of the sick-minded elitist society that had hurt her family so much and that she now despised.

Five months later Hassan got a job in Zakar, an old city in the north of the Middle East. Zaib had never heard of the place. She imagined the desert would be dull and depressing and she got a sinking feeling just thinking about it. The Middle East in general sparked images of the history of the Arabs as she imagined it, *Bedouins* in their black tents with several wives and children, travelling across baking desert plains on tired camels in the searing heat. She saw empty streets and yellow lights, big Chevrolets and people talking in a language she couldn't understand.

'Can't we just stay here?' she asked Hassan.

'Zaib, this is my future, it's my career. You want me to do well, don't you?'

They had to start packing immediately. Daddy's things had already been put away by his son, Muhammad, Zaib's stepbrother. He and Saima had come to attend their father's funeral and they had left, with most of his things. It was the least they could claim of their father, his *things*. They met Zaib briefly. She hugged her stepsister, who seemed to appreciate the gesture but withdrew quickly. She longed more than ever to meet auntie Fatima. She knew she had to do it before leaving.

Fatima was now over eighty. Zaib travelled to Peshawar a week before leaving for Zakar, where she lived. She was greeted by the family with an odd mixture of affection and disdain. Fatima was in a wheel chair and could hardly speak. She could see that the years had not been kind to her. She had deep wrinkles on her forehead and her eyes looked like two hollow caves. Her mouth drooped at the corners and there was a sadness all around her that pained Zaib deeply. She almost ran to her and held her tightly. For Zaib she was a part of her father's life and history and she was a woman who had been hurt and jilted, whose world had been cruelly snatched away from her. She was punished for doing nothing wrong, and there was no justice in that. Relatives had told her that she loved Shafi even after he had left her. She had insisted that her children talk about him with the utmost respect and it was her wish that they try and build a relationship with their stepsisters Zaib and Devika. But mummy never let that happen. She was too jealous, too possessive, too self-centred to let them in.

She looked at Fatima closely. Fatima and her father had started their journey long before she had even existed or her mother even knew daddy. After the divorce, Shafi would visit once or twice a month to see his children. Under pressure from Zaib's mother the visits became less and less frequent. During her life she prayed regularly, never forgetting to thank God for his blessings. Now looking at this tiny thin bony figure in front of her, Zaib hugged her tightly, the tears rolled down her cheeks. Fatima looked at her and tilted her head to one side, staring at her hard. She looked surprised at first and then she smiled and put her hand on Zaib's head. She saw recognition. It was the hand of God. Zaib had the blessing she was looking for. She was, at last, ready for the new world she was about to step into.

When they were finally about to leave for Zakar, Zaib started to grieve for her city, the city where her father lived and died, where his trees still breathed his words and mummy came out occasionally to hang the clothes out for drying or to marvel at her beautiful mansion, with her hands on her hips and her head held high. The scent of mangoes filled the air like the smell of rain. Ghazala sang her songs in some corner of the city and the flowers she had picked for daddy so carefully were imbedded in her city's throbbing grounds, the rebirth of roses imminent. She searched desperately for all that she was about to lose, but then she knew deep inside that those things could never really be lost. She stroked the memory of those long gone looked up towards the sky and smiled.

ꟃ

7

Devika

If only Devi khala was here, thought Alya. But she couldn't even tell her. How could she? Devi had had her third nervous breakdown less than six months ago, besides it was usually Zaib who helped Devi out of her depression, not the other way round. Would Devi khala have the strength to see her *little* sister like this? The sister she had nurtured and adored all her life, the sister she had such high hopes for.

Devika, named after her Hindu aunt from her father's side (Shafi's father was half-Hindu, half-Muslim, but only the Muslim side was passed on to him and no one ever referred to his father's 'Hindu' side), was Zaib's only sister. As a child, Zaib shared the bed with Devika, always wrapping her legs firmly around her in case she disappeared in the middle of the night. She nuzzled close to her sister at night for comfort. The two spent much time talking about how perfect nature's creations were, about ice-cream waves in the sky and twittering wrens who filled the trees at dusk to feed their babies. They studied the different types of veins and colours on various species of flowers and leaves and wondered how God could think up of so much variety. They watched birds feed their young and marveled at how much love there was in the world. They discussed religious mythologies. Devi read avidly about the Greek gods, about Venus and Persephone, Pluto and Neptune and their amazing adventures and how they won wars for love and power. She saw Narcissus in her dreams, more beautiful than a million diamond forests with sapphire trees and she saw Aurora causing the first rustle that gently wakes babies on 'ruby' mornings from their deep slumber.

Devi told her stories from the New Testament and from the Quran describing in vivid detail the miracles that the prophets had performed. The story that stuck the most in Zaib's mind was the one in which people were throwing stones at two adulterers ('adulterers' were people who Devi said loved each other but were not married) and Christ stops them saying: 'Let him who is without sin cast the First Stone.' Devi explained to her that the story was about love and forgiveness and about being good to one another. Zaib remembered all the lessons her sister taught her and listened to her intently as she told her each story. She once asked Devi why there weren't prophets anymore. She wondered where all those great gods and prophets had gone. Devi told her that the prophets had been ordered to come to earth by god and that god had sent them to teach the world the path of truth and honesty. She said their time had now passed because they had important work to do in heaven. 'They did what they came for and left, Zaib. There is a *purpose* for *everything in life.*' Usually on weekends Zaib and Devi played music on their small transistor and danced. Zaib wore imitation jewellery pretending she was a dancing girl, while Devi sang her favourite tunes and clapped. She went round and round in circles with her multi-coloured *dupattas* caressing the wind with their soft fabric, while Devi encouraged her to keep going laughing and singing along.

Zaib would often recall one particular red June day when she sat chatting with Devi under a lemon tree. They laughed about the green bird shit dropping on their heads and discussed their parents' weird-looking friends and made fun of their hairstyles and their funny clothes. The air smelt of juicy lemons and Devi had just started telling her about a new book she was reading called, *Oliver Twist* as part of her 'O' level course, when someone rang the bell at the gate. Before Devi could stop her, Zaib ran out to open it. There in front of her stood her friend from school Nusrat, smiling proudly. But Nusrat was not Nusrat anymore. She had chopped all her hair off! Zaib started shouting, 'Get out! Get out immediately! You are not my friend anymore, you have become a boy.' She then picked up a stick and started chasing her around the garden until the poor girl was so terrified she ran away. Devi came running out, but by that time the girl had left. Zaib turned to Devi, 'But why did she have to do that, she looks just like a boy!' Devi had often teased Zaib about that incident when they were older.

One afternoon two years later, Zaib came back from school to find Devika packing a suitcase. She asked her where she was going.

'Zaib I was going to tell you. Honey, as you know there is no school that offers 'A' levels in Lahore and so mummy and daddy went to see a school in Reading in England last summer. It is an excellent school and it means I will probably get good grades and then end up going to a really good university in England. Zaib, you know it has always been my dream to study in England.'

'But you didn't tell me!'

'Zaib, we weren't sure. I just found out.'

'I hate you!'

'I am scared too Zaib, you have to be supportive.'

She had betrayed her. 'Devi, don't go or if you really have to take me too!'

'We can't leave our parents alone Zaib, besides I will keep coming back for holidays and time will pass so quickly, I'll be back before you know it.'

It was like crawling through a black tunnel and not knowing when it's going to end. All Zaib could think of was ways of stopping Devi from going and she refused to speak to her. On the day she was leaving Zaib didn't go to the airport to see her off. Devi hugged her tightly sobbing before leaving, 'Pray for my success Zaib. I'll be back soon. And be strong for mummy, she will need you even more after I am gone.'

No matter what she did, Devi had to leave and Zaib could do nothing to stop her. She cried until her eyes hurt and refused to go to school for three days after Devi left. Her sister phoned from England every week but Zaib refused to speak to her – in the beginning. Gradually she was able to squeeze a few words out. But there was no real respite for Zaib and little meaning to her life until she had met Ghazala, a year later…

Two years passed and though the pain was less, she ached for her sister. It was as if a part of her was missing. Every day she imagined what they would do when she saw her next a million times.

One still hot day when the crows were hovering around the garden indiscriminately, still not satiated with the morning leftovers, Zaib was told Devika was arriving. Until now she knew nothing about her sister's imminent arrival. Why hadn't anybody told her? She almost cried with excitement when her mother broke the news to her. She started getting dressed immediately, throwing her clothes around the room frantically. 'Oh mummy I can't decide what to wear!'

'Zaib, that blue dress looks lovely.'

'I'll wear my red *shalwar kameez* with the *gotey walla dupatta*.'

'Ok whatever you want Zaib. But hurry up we are getting late.'

Devi was coming home for her first vacation! She could hardly speak. The house was brimming with the dripping smell of tuberoses and fried food. Zaib rushed to her sister's room to make sure everything was neat and tidy. Then she jumped into the car and off they went to pick her up from the airport. When they arrived they were told the flight was delayed. 'Trust PIA,' her mother said. They had to wait two more hours, but when Devi finally came through the sliding glass doors, Zaib felt a strange lightness that was new to her. She ran towards her, aching to hold her sister in her arms, though a little cautious and slightly shy of the new, perhaps changed Devi.

What if the outside world had changed her somehow? Maybe Devi expected a different kind of welcome. Zaib was nervous. But Devi was exactly the same. A bit taller maybe, she thought. She almost lifted Zaib up, hugging and kissing her profusely.

Her mother smiled at her affectionately and hugged her, 'How was the flight beta?'

'A little tiring,' came the short reply. Devi had done well academically. She had always been studious, keen not to disappoint her teachers and parents, and she passed her 'A' levels with two A's and a B. It secured her a place to study English at Queens' College, Oxford and she had come home for the summer before joining university in September. Her parents had thrown a party to celebrate. Mummy was glittering with diamonds, shuttling her daughter from guest to guest, as if she were a shining new ornament. Devi who was shy by nature and who disliked the extra attention, felt embarrassed. When she tried to stop her mother, she got an irritated reaction, 'For God's sake Devi, do behave yourself, after all this is a big achievement. *Log mubarik dena chahtey hein.*'

Zaib always called the drawing room, the 'crystal room'. Crystal proliferated and spread like water in mummy's lounge. Mummy loved crystal. But to Zaib crystal made the lounge look clinical and scarred, as a dead butterfly once did when she looked closely at it as a child dispelling the myth of a butterfly being almost a mythical creature in its perfect beauty. The lounge was a mysterious place for her; she used to watch mummy's and daddy's guests making jokes among the crystal from the adjoining dining room window: it was easy to hide there because she could not be seen. The guests were ghosts, permeating the objects around them with their easy-going fluid movements. She saw the men in a cloudy haze blowing smoke rings in the air, their shiny heads and white teeth glistening under lounge moonlight. Women stared at each other with hatred fixing their hair constantly, flirting with each other's husbands outrageously. Her mother floated around the room like a helium balloon about to burst with joy using her famous charm that could melt the most hardened of individuals. Zaib had usually wanted all the guests to leave but when they were actually gone, for some odd reason, she longed to see them again.

Within hours of arriving home, the sisters felt as if they had never been apart. They talked until the early hours of the morning and when they finally went to sleep Zaib felt at peace at last. For the next three months they were inseparable, discussing their future plans, their aspirations and their dreams. Zaib wanted to become a writer and Devi wanted to become a social worker, helping set up homes for orphans. Zaib told her nothing of Ghazala, as if her memory was too pure for her to discuss her even with Devi. It didn't seem to be a choice, but more just a natural instinct to keep to herself what was sacred between herself and her first love; there was no room for anyone else in that space.

This time when Devi left it was much harder. Her absence weighed heavily on Zaib, the ache was far greater and with Ghazala gone, there was no one she could trust enough to comfort her. She drifted further away from her mother, secretly blaming her for taking her away from Ghazala. Maybe if she had been there instead of in Nathia Gali, Ghazala would still be there. *She and I in our womb bed.*

The next three years went by slowly, with Devi not being able to visit at all. It was the beginning of a dwindling career for their father and he couldn't afford to send her money for the air ticket, so Devi had to stay back throughout her degree program. At times Zaib thought her life was gradually being sucked out of her. The green table lamp they had both shared for all those years, gave her a foreboding glare and Zaib sometimes sat for hours trying on Devi's clothes and play acting in her room. It made her feel closer to her sister, but it just wasn't enough.

Finally, when Devi came back it took time for her to accept the change.

She eyed her sister suspiciously in the beginning. Was she more English now? Did she still love her as much? Had anyone taken her place?

But time told her that it was all the same. Even ten wouldn't have made a difference. The most difficult part was over. She was back with her again.

They talked about Oxford and Devi's long romance with the city of 'love and learning' as she called it. Devi told Zaib about people she met, the experiences she had. It opened up a world of wonders for Zaib and she probed Devi about her professors, her teachers, her friends. Devi seemed most impressed by her Metaphysical Poetry professor, Kerry, whom she said she respected immensely. She seemed taken up by her artistic temperament and her courage to say what she believed in even if it offended or annoyed others. Zaib felt a tinge of jealousy.

'Was she pretty? What did you do together?'

'Yes, she is sort of pretty, green eyes and delicate features, she is sort of voluptuous like the women in old paintings, she reminds me of that woman in "Flaming June", that's the best way I can describe her. She wears very colourful clothes that never match but still seem to go together really well, in a strange way.'

Devi told Zaib one story after another, gesticulating wildly and jumping from one thing to another. She tried to pack in as many stories as she could in one day, while the latter listened with her chin on her palm and her eyes wide with excitement, hungry for more, anxious to learn about her sister's adventures, the other world being something akin to Alice's wonderland, but without the fear. Some of the things her sister said about her courses, Zaib didn't understand, but she didn't want to look foolish in front of Devi, so she pretended she understood, while Devi carried on, lost in her past, holding on to all that she had seen, so that she could keep it safe inside her. There was so much to absorb, to never let go of.

Devi was still talking when mummy walked in smiling.

'Aren't you girls hungry? It's almost ten.'

They both looked at her, visibly annoyed, but they got up and went to the dining table where they sat obediently and ate quietly. They hardly touched their food. That night they slept at three in the morning, underneath lilac clouds in a snow topped sky.

Zaib had stared at her sister's face resisting sleep a long time after Devi had dozed off. At last things were right again.

❧

A year passed and Zaib had noticed that something about Devi had changed. It made her feel caged because she couldn't understand what it was. Devi looked constantly distracted.

'Zaib, come bring me your *paranda*, I'll make your plait.'

Zaib sat down on the floor in front of her while she separated the strands of her hair in three parts, looking at each one with unnatural concentration.

She spoke suddenly, 'Zaib, will you meet someone for me? I met him a few months ago. I love him a lot and we want to get married.' She ended the sentence quickly as if without thought.

Zaib screamed, 'Aow, Devi don't pull so hard, my head hurts!'

Zaib could barely face another separation from her sister and even the mention of a stranger; she could not tolerate an intruder in their lives. His name was Haider and he was studying law. He was the son of a *well-respected* businessman in the community and Devi had been meeting him secretly for the last three months. Once again Zaib felt betrayed.

'You could have told me.'

'I didn't know how to.'

With the inclusion of Haider in their lives, Devi started staring at all sorts of objects vacantly for long periods of time. She also listened to old Indian Rafi and Mukesh songs incessantly and gazed at the world as if it was all new to her, as if every time it offered her a new version of itself, in which she got lost.

The altered Devi irritated Zaib and she refused to meet him at first, unwilling to accept his existence in their lives. But Devi was insistent and finally after much persuasion from Devi, she agreed. After all Devi said she loved him and apart from being curious she wanted to make sure he was 'right' for her sister. They arranged to meet on a day when their parents were out. He came in from the back entrance so that the servants wouldn't see him. Devi quickly ushered him into her room, where Zaib sat waiting. The instant she saw him, there was a strong dislike. He reminded her of one of the lazy gnomes Ralph had told her about when she was younger, the one who slept all the time, never waking up in time to help with floods and earthquakes that frequently took place in gnome land, forever late, forever unequipped to deal with such unexpected eventualities. He had green eyes and he was tall. That was it. Devi had always had a thing for coloured eyes. He spoke with an almost British accent and seemed intelligent, but there was an infectious apathy about him that irked her. Besides, for Zaib, her sister was far superior in every way and she had expected her to do better. But then she saw that expression in Devi's eyes whenever she looked at him. It could only be described as complete devotion and even Zaib couldn't deny the truth of it to herself. Every time he spoke or even moved Devi watched him with so much hope and trust in her eyes that Zaib knew that all that mattered was that right now her sister loved this man, and her opinion of him was of little consequence to anything that was important. So she started to help them meet in the garden and occasionally to go out together, guarding them in case someone saw and made a scandal of it, or in case mummy and daddy saw them and created a scene. Zaib gave them the danger signal by whistling when her parents' car pulled up in the porch or when someone came too close to the main gate of the house. That was Haider's cue to jump over the back wall and disappear.

Initially, Devi looked constantly animated and was full of energy but after some time Zaib noticed that her sister looked increasingly uneasy. She caught her crying in bed at night several times and finally asked her what was wrong. Devi told her she wanted to marry Haider, but that he hadn't proposed. She couldn't bear to see her sister in so much pain.

Once, while Haider was waiting for Devi in the garden, Zaib went up to him, 'If you want to be with my sister you have to marry her, otherwise my parents say you can't see her anymore.' Devi caught the last part of her sentence while coming out of the house. She turned to Haider, embarrassed and said, 'She is just joking, please ignore her.' then raised her hand to Zaib as if she was going to smack her on her shoulder. Zaib ran into the house and hid behind the cupboard of her bedroom.

Almost six months passed and Haider had still not proposed marriage to Devi. She had lost weight and generally looked weak. It was of course unheard of for a girl to suggest marriage to a boy, but too much time had passed and Devi finally decided she had to take matters into her own hands. So she asked him the next time they met.

'You must ask your parents about us soon Haider. You are serious about us, aren't you?'

Haider had been avoiding the inevitable, but not because he didn't want to marry her. That had not even occurred to him, it was simply that life was easier this way and he somehow acted as if they could go on as they were for some time to come. Marriage was definitely on the cards but as far as he was concerned for now they were so happy they would simply just not think of it. But he could see that that was no longer possible.

'Of course I want a family, and children, a home too.'

Haider saw the severity in her big eyes.

'Tomorrow then, I will tell them tomorrow. Wait for me in the evening around 7 and I'll let you know how it went. Don't worry, everything will be alright.'

That night neither sister slept well.

ঔ

Haider watched a leaf lying on the road for several minutes, willing it not to move, as if his life depended on it. Eventually the wind took it somewhere secret, in a hollow that escaped his scope of vision. He walked on, bruised, unable to reclaim the leaf as his own. He stopped at the bank of the river Ravi and sat next to a willow hoping somehow he could hide within it, or escape to land or water and erase the time of his creation. While contemplating his *sin* he chewed on a blade of grass. He had thought about it all night and knew how his mother would react to Devika, now it was just a case of going through the motions. But then again maybe he was wrong, maybe she had some mercy left in her, maybe her love for her son would override all else and change things. He would try. He would try hard. There would be a confrontation, the inevitable clash of wills and then eventually the ennui of life would seep in, always there, finding its way into the small clefts left unnoticed, killing you bit by bit, until the final stumble into death. A fly rubbed its hands planning his future with every rub and he knew that he was unable to break away from the apathy covering his existence like a blanket. He turned towards the liquid gold hay field behind him, his body undulating to the evening bee ready to sting or die. Had he been dishonest to both women? Had he simply been buying time? As his shame broke the hum, he covered his face with his hands and then looked up at the sky. With his eyes towards heaven and God on his tongue he tried to save himself.

'Help me God.'

When he woke up the following morning, the air around him made him nauseous. He walked out of his room looking for ammi. It had to be done now or he would never be able to do it. Ammi was paaned up in the living room, sitting on a green and gold divan, like Cleopatra and a plan. The silver *paan* box placed neatly in her hand told Haider that he had to do it soon, before she laid out the green leaf and laced it with the thick brown liquid, sprinkling silver *chalia* and a sugar-like substance on it. She wrapped it up quickly, folding it neatly, corner to corner and put the *paan* in her mouth, savouring every bite. Now he was sure he would lose his courage. He thought she sensed what was coming by the way she rolled the folded green leaf filled with *kimaam* in her mouth, the new one in the making, her red mouth munching away.

'Ammi, did you have your breakfast this morning? You look a little pale.'

'Haan *beta*, but I think my blood pressure has dropped again, I must go to the doctor and have it checked.' She was a merciless hypochondriac with a will to live that was stronger than most.

'Ammi, I was thinking it would be better if I got married now. You know now that I am almost done with my studies.'

'Oh thank God, my son has finally come to his senses!!! I will go to Munira's straight away.'

She seemed genuinely excited and he experienced a premature guilt.

'Ammi, I want to marry a girl of my choice, times have changed, and anyway I don't even know Munira. I was only ten when we were engaged!' Munira was his first cousin.

'What do you mean? We never marry out of the family, you know that.'

She said this with true disbelief rather than to convince him.

'Please ammi, times have changed. I have met a bright and beautiful girl and I love her.'

Her face went red. 'How dare you say such things in front of your mother!'

He was choking between her words. His mother had married his father when she was barely thirteen. He was the youngest of three children, two boys and the eldest, a sister. Mahvish, his sister was born when his mother was fourteen. The child was born brain damaged and for years after that his mother had been depressed, spending her days caring for the child and hardly meeting anyone. At the age of ten the child had died of complications related to pneumonia. His father had made it clear that he believed the girl had died of some sort of neglect and his mother had carried the guilt with her throughout her life. It had made her bitter and hard, but Haider had instinctively protected her from the judging eyes of her in-laws and the cruelty of his father's hurtful words. He was at pains to prove what a good mother she was by praising her at every opportunity and being an obedient and loving son. He even fought the natural feelings of rebelliousness that come with adolescence and followed a course for his life set by his mother and the consequences of Mahvish's death: Munira was a part of that course, as were her dreams of Haider becoming a big lawyer and making the family *proud*. Now sitting in front of her dwarfed by their opulent surroundings, it dawned on him that there really was nothing much he had done for himself, in fact he wasn't even sure what he had really wanted throughout his life. Where in all this was *his* plan? Asking for Devi was the first time he had asked for anything at all. Surely she would see that and soften. But her expression told him he had to push harder.

'Ammi, it is not fair. I love her.' His voice sounded alien to him, sounded like it was failing. She got up and walked out.

They spoke about it again a few hours later, when his mother knocked on his bedroom door and walked in. He felt he was on safer ground, until she sat down on the bed. Such close proximity to his mother made him uncomfortable.

'Who is she?'

'You know the renowned lawyer, Mr Shafi. His daughter.'

It was too hard for her to bear. The horror of what would happen to their family flashed through her eyes and she swallowed hard as she spoke, unable to move her body. This would be it, he thought, his relationship with his mother would be permanently altered by a betrayal she thought she did not deserve, and he knew he was guilty of.

'Over my dead body. Never. You will not do this to me. The daughter of that Chr... woman.' She stood up with difficulty, holding on to a chair next to the bed for support, and walked to the door. Just before leaving, she turned around slowly and looked at him for a moment. It was a look of a thousand tales, those of her pain over the years, a mother's warm embrace, her loneliness, her sadness, her constant efforts to prove herself a worthy mother, and much much more, emotions that did not have a face but a meaning that only he could share with her. Finally, there was a plea, a plea that said please don't put me through the stigma; don't kill me before I am dead.

It was at that moment he gave her up instantly, with the knowledge that it would cost him years, maybe the rest of his years, but there was simply nothing else he could do.

☙❧

The morning Haider had told Devi he was going to talk to his parents, she had prayed all day, her face buried in her hands. There was an old book lying in front of her, a leather-bound oracle with frayed edges and a wrinkled midriff. Devi had inherited it from her great-grandfather and she often smelt its pages for comfort. She recited verses from the book, turning the pages delicately, in case they disintegrated between her fingers. She felt she could touch its wisdom in the gold rim of this ancient scroll. She kept praying and pacing the room. Zaib was close by though she knew better than to disturb her. Mummy and daddy had not come back from work yet. The doorbell rang. It was Haider. Devi looked at him expectantly. Zaib was standing close by though out of their vision. He didn't speak for a few seconds.

'What did they say Haider?'

'Devi, they said if I marry you, they would never see me again.'

☙❧

For a long time after he had left her, she still held the belief that he still loved her. 'He had no choice' was what she kept repeating to Zaib. A few more months and the bitterness set in. 'Who would want to marry into such a scandalous family anyway,' she'd say to Zaib. Her sins were in her blood, she had inherited them. 'This is God's way of punishing us.' Zaib didn't want to upset her so she kept quiet most of the time and bit back her tears.

One day she was particularly upset after mummy and daddy had attended a church service. 'See they don't care about what people will say. They are still the most notorious couple in the community and it is us who have to pay the price. I hate them!' The blame and the hatred seemed to consume her and carried on for months. All sorts of things came out of her mouth, 'Father thinks he is a saint. He has killed us with his hedonistic principles. All he cares about is his life.' This time Zaib could not hold back. 'Devi please, he adores us, you know that and you know how much he goes through for this family.' But Devi just kept arguing until eventually Zaib became increasingly worried about Devi's mental state. She didn't want to worry her father so she chose to confide in her mother for a change.

'What do we do, she is so angry and upset?'

Her mother was calm and focused, 'Well I think the only thing we can do is to get her married. We have someone in mind. He's a major in the army. Let's see, we are meeting his parents next week.'

She was probably right. Anything was better than this, maybe this was the best thing for her.

It took six months to prepare for Devi's marriage to a man they hardly knew, during which time she hardly spoke to either of her parents. After the wedding Devi moved to Multan within days, where her husband was stationed. As far as Zaib was concerned they had all lost Devi to a man who had nothing to do with them, *an outsider*. It was all arranged in such a hurry that Zaib had no time to get to know him. After Devi left, it was as if mummy had read her mind, 'I know why you are worried, but he is educated and intelligent she needed this. She will get busy in making her home now. Give her some time in her new life.' And that was what they did; they gave her time until a year later when Zaib received an urgent telegram from Devi asking her to visit immediately.

All of it chipping away at Zaib, incessantly, meticulously….

Zaib was stirring again. It was time to call the doctor.

What happened? What happened to the flowers, please someone tell me! Someone… Where is my love?

❧

8

Devi's Faith

'Hello, can I speak to Dr Rizwi? It's urgent.'

It was a bad line and Alya could barely hear the woman on the other end. She raised her voice, 'Should I call back?' The woman had already banged the phone.

'Damn it. Typical.'

She called back. 'Can I speak to Dr Rizwi?'

'He is not in town. He will be back tomorrow evening.'

Alya looked back at her mother anxiously and held the receiver tightly. She heard the second click on the other end of the phone. She couldn't even change doctors at this stage; he was the only one her mother trusted and the only one who knew her, the old Zaib, the new Zaib, all the Zaibs that had existed in the last twenty years. *Twenty years.* Twenty years ago when the first sign of trouble began, was when Dr Rizwi first came into the picture.

Five years earlier, the Shafi family had summoned Dr Rizwi once again.

'Zaib, you don't have to worry, I am here to help.'

Zaib had looked at him suspiciously, 'Who is this man?'

The question had been directed to Sonia. Sonia, who always looked in control even when she wasn't, answered almost immediately. 'Ammi, he is your doctor and he is here to help.'

'Help with what? I don't need his help.'

'He is here to help us all, not just you, in fact he is here to help me and Alya more than anyone else.'

Zaib had fallen into deep thought as if struck by some distant memory that she wanted to latch onto. All the other things happening around her were unimportant for now.

Dr Rizwi left soon afterwards only to return early in the morning the next day. Dr Rizwi had always been a great influence on ammi (even though ammi was not recognizing him at the moment) and a dependable shoulder for the rest of the family. Except Alya. She mistrusted anyone too close to ammi.

He had started with, 'Zaib, can you tell me where Hassan is?'

Alya almost threw him out. How could he? What was he thinking? Was he insane or just simply cruel?

He repeated, 'Zaib, can you tell me where Hassan is?'

Alya took the first step towards him, when she felt Sonia's hand on her arm. She looked up at her. Sonia's eyes looked severe – *don't*, they said.

'But you know he can't.'

'Alya, don't. Let him do his job,' she said.

At that point Dr Rizwi had asked the girls to leave. 'I think we should be left alone now. Can you please leave quietly?'

How could Alya trust this butcher with her mother? He was going to kill her. Sonia almost pulled Alya outside, 'Come on we have to go now.'

'But what if she....'

Sonia cut her off, 'She can't be any worse off then she was before he came here. Let him do what he thinks is right. He knows her too.'

Dr Rizwi emerged after two hours.

'She is sleeping now. I would like to talk to both of you. Can you come to my clinic this evening? I have to go right now, there's a patient waiting for me. For now just let her be. Don't ask too many questions and let her talk as much as she wants to and about anything she wants to.' Alya looked into his soft brown eyes and remembered the chocolate éclair candies he used to give them when they were children. She felt ashamed at doubting him.

'Will she get through this?'

'Yes, inshallah if we all cooperate with her and with each other. Try not to panic. Ok?'

That was the beginning of a long and arduous journey for them all.

ঙ৪৯

When Zaib and Hassan arrived in Zakar she found the heat stifling. Inside a ball of searing air, the heat stung her face and the humidity made it difficult to breathe. *She saw Devi again and again, about to leave for England.* The vast desert plains seemed deathly to her. Hassan was anxious to make her comfortable. He tried to reassure her, 'Zaib, you'll get used to it, it's only a matter of time. After all we had nothing left in Lahore.'

'Nothing is a big word Hassan.'

He was right. Initially she used her imagination to make it more bearable for herself. With time it took on a face of its own.

The smooth desert sands became elusive and proud and she began to make love to them. She found the dunes alluring like the indulgent curves of a woman's body and she buried herself inside them. She chased bronze fairies with raven black hair and mysterious eyes telling her life had more secrets in the drum beat of the desert than among the whisper of trees. They showed her the splendour of love and lust, with the knowledge that there are no limits in God's design. At other times, in the calm of a warm breeze, she found a new tranquility in the trail of red ants, denting the dunes with their judicious feet. She marveled at colourful insects carrying their troubles on their backs and their wounds in their hearts. She experienced the sea for the first time and was fascinated by its chameleon lure. She would stand at the harbor where a salt zephyr caressed the fisherman's net while the regal fisherman stretched his arms displaying the contours of a perfect body, blackened by the sun, his glistening ribs projecting the strength of a master of his art. Zaib saw her father's footprints on the sand and heard her mother's voice in the ruffles of the sea. She would wait for the crabs to emerge at sunset and watch their pinkness permeate the skin of the beach until it was time for them to return home to the vast blue in front of her. And the *azaan* ... ever soothing ever comforting ... brushed the sparkling sands with its sweet odour.

ઌ૪ઌ

The company Hassan worked for had arranged for their accommodation. It was a large white bungalow. It looked like a square block of sugar served at hotels in china bowls with hot drinks. A brand new Citroen stood in the porch, a metallic olive structure with an inflated belly and a pretentious grin. Zaib felt like she had been transported back to her parents' crystal room. Was there no escape from all these monster fears that these things seemed to emanate in this small world? She squeezed herself into a ball and used the walls of her new house as a temporary resting place. Whenever she could she would get away to the sea or the dunes.

She and Hassan had only been in Zakar two weeks when a letter from Devika arrived. 'What's wrong this time?'

Hassan was a sympathetic man but when it came to protecting Zaib, he could be brutal.

'Zaib, she needs to handle it herself, whatever it is.'

'She needs me. I have to go to her, immediately. He has left her again and run off with some whore!'

'But we've just moved Zaib, doesn't she understand she has to ...'

Zaib cut him off. 'What do you mean *she* has to? She has to *what*? You know what she's been going through, how can you be so ruthless?'

'Ruthless! That's just so amazing Zaib. She's the one who is ruthless; for God's sake let her handle it herself.'

'I don't remember you being like this.'

'Just come back in one piece and sane!'

Devi's driver was there to collect her from the airport. She sat in the car and turned to the driver, 'What's your name?'

'Shaukat, baaji.'

'How is mem saab?'

'Not too well baaji. But she talks about you a lot so we are all happy you are here.'

'When is saab coming home?'

'No one knows baaji.'

They were both quiet for the rest of the journey.

Devi's maid, Rubina, answered the door. She had inherited Rubina from her parents.

Zaib felt a pain in her chest when she saw her and hugged her tightly for several minutes. She was so relieved to see a familiar face, a face from home. 'How are you? How are the children?'

Rubina's eyes moistened. 'Baaji, I am just so glad to see you. Please don't leave us any time soon.'

'Is it that bad?'

'Yes baaji.'

She took her to the bedroom. Zaib's hands started to sweat. She had not felt this nervous the last time she had visited Devi, but the circumstances were different then.

Devi was in bed repeating a dua over and over again.

'Devi, it's me.'

'Who?'

Zaib walked up to her bed slowly. 'Devi, I just arrived. How are you feeling?'

'Is that you Zaib? I think I've found my place, my cave is safe.'

'You must come and live with me in Zakar for a while, the sea is beautiful.'

'A yellow bud in Flora's tomb.'

'Like dried flowers in books.'

'Was I really wearing pink lipstick when that picture was taken? Why do I have lipstick on? I was only seven or eight. They touch them up so much, don't they? Zaib you must start believing, he is watching us all the time you know.'

She became fuzzy and tinsel-like-thread in her head about where to fit the events into each other. Memories are cardboard clean, but pictures lie.

The pictures are not yellow yet darling (as you may think), just torn at the edges through neglect.

'Everyone believes in God, Devi, even atheists believe in God.'

She looked distracted, 'Did you ever climb that beanstalk in the end?'

'I climbed it with Ghazala.'

'But not with me.'

'What did you find?'

'Enough to write a book about nothing.'

'I can't hear you. I think they are here.'

Dried flowers rolled down her wrist.

She seemed to be burrowing for food in her bed like a squirrel in warm places where pin head eyes pluck blue-green discs from peacock's wings dislodging the order of Devi's zigzag mind to breed a puss ball cloud as an emblem of love. Her purple vein had spread its legs tap tap dance like this and like that, cartwheel Devi, a star for the stars, blinking blinking, the skull of an onion breaking, breaking for the vein to turn murky where only the Styx knows why. When the hare popped up, Oh Zaib how I love Alice with her feet twisted round watching a lamp-less bulb unwrapping the spine of her wooden bed crossing out the lines of verses stitched to the seams muffling the breath of soap screened sheets. I have killed her in my dreams so she can save herself from God to see the needles in the hands of pinhead men, feeding her fish shit in a bowl cracking under the folding milk sky with one spot of blood crawling beneath the surface of carved saints with bits of words in her pillows and shoes where blue dust bakes with God in their soles.

Devi and Zaib were interrupted by a swarm of bee-like creatures buzzing, conspiring amongst themselves. Dressed in black, they were the dacoits of love. They had come to deliver something to Devi, something Zaib would not forget. Suddenly the sharp whiff of *itar* laced the room. Zaib felt sick, the smell reminded her of slimy green seaweed on Zakar beaches in the burning heat of the summer. The bees sat down on the floor around the bed.... bzzzzzzzzzzzzzzzzz. Presently the howling began.

'Begum sahiba, what has happened to you! *Au khudaya*, what have you done to yourself!!! We will pray for you *begum sahiba, inshallah* God will bestow health upon you once again.'

Another one, 'God almighty the all merciful will bless you.'

Then almost in unison, 'God will help our baaji.'

One by one they continued in the same sing-song manner until one of them burst into a loud wailing. She wailed and wailed and wailed above the sound of the matchstickmen in corners. Devika was holding Zaib's hand tight, she kept her from reacting to them, she told her in her silence not to move, it was a warning. She heard the seconds, one, two, three, four... daddy? Where are you?

'Ssshhh, bibi is trying to sleep now,' Rubina tried to stop them.

Devi left Zaib's hand and trying to sit up, said, 'No, no, I am awake bring tea for everyone.'

Rubina left reluctantly.

The bees were not going to stop, until people died, until the head stones piled up one at a time so they could wail even louder.

Tea came with biscuits. Zaib remembered them pecking away, like ravens devouring almost ever last crumb, the few that escaped landed in the clutches of a hungry ant pacing the vicinity of bee land. They ate. They gnawed the biscuits – vulture on a carcass. One let out a proud burp, 'We will pray for you everyday. Where is sahib?'

Zaib could have snatched her eyes out; she could have ripped open her brains. How could they? They knew... they knew what he was doing to her, the bitches. For Devi she sat still, her heart pounding. Devi closed her eyes more tightly, this time whispering a prayer. Her bandaged arms smelt of metholated spirit.

Judgement Day had arrived and no one knew. A while of that and then a drawing of the curtains. But there was no applause in that room. Zaib watched Devi while Devi smiled politely at them and asked them to come again. Devi had made a choice, a choice she *believed* in. Zaib, on the other hand, felt she was without choices, losing the one woman she loved more than life itself. She felt like an eagle standing at the edge of the universe with nowhere to go.

☙

Two months later Zaib was back at her sister's side.

Zaib had been told her sister was 'behaving in an unstable manner'. She was watching the moon of *her* city from the window, wondering what the next few years were going to bring her. She carried a steady sadness with her now. Hassan was so far way. She imagined he was dreaming of her. Then she saw a bottle crash on the floor and a loud bang coming from Devi's room. The woodpecker pecked at her door. *Devi is dead. Tick tock, tick, tock, Devi is dead* – this time in a sing-song manner. Then there was a chorus of voices, all from Devi's room. Her legs trembled like when mummy used to scream at daddy, as she walked towards Devi. She was not in her bed. Devi? There was a cackling noise behind her. She shuddered and turned around. Devi was sitting on a chair looking like Miss Havisham. Her hair fell in wild strands in front of her face. Devi?

Mummy said I could have that new dolly for Christmas if I want and you can't stop! Nanny nanny boo boo nanny nanny boo boo!!! I will get the doll and you won't get anything, nanny nanny boo boo nanny nanny boo boo!!!! Has mummy come home from work yet? Mummy go work now, Zaib go schooool, I play with my dolly. Has mummy come home yet? I have to take ten rupees to school tomorrow for our picnic... ... .

Zaib was transfixed with terror. Zaib had never seen her sister so frail. Please Devi, please the crows have left their feast, come home Devi. Devi would never come back and Zaib saw her rotting away in an asylum. She picked up the phone, shaking. The receiver slipped from her hand and fell.

Don't break mummy's vase Zaib, she loves that vase.

She found the phone book and called Devi's psychiatrist. She was asleep. The guard was not helpful, 'For God's sake wake her up, my sister needs her!'

Mummy has come home Zaib?

The chaukidaar finally woke her up and Zaib told her what had happened. When she arrived Devi had been a child for over an hour and Zaib thought she'd lost her forever. The doctor pretended Devi was really a child by speaking to her firmly, gently. Gradually Devi started using a more adult tone. When she was with them again, Zaib sat by her for the rest of the night. *A shoal of fish washed ashore dead weeds of long ago. And the craving woodpecker still pecked.* The next day Devi was the same; she remembered nothing and no one told her. All Zaib kept thinking was that next time there would be no coming back.

When she returned to Zakar, Hassan saw fear in Zaib's eyes.

'What was it this time?' He asked indifferently.

'How can you be so callous Hassan?'

'What is her therapist or psychiatrist, whoever it is doing with all that money?'

'No one can prevent something like that from happening, you know that.'

Two years later Devi suffered yet another nervous breakdown, but this time Zaib wasn't there. Gradually, Devi's health started to deteriorate and Zaib found herself more and more powerless to help her sister.

It had all started with one telegram. Alya, who had been quite fond of her khaloo, was surprised.

A year after Devi's marriage to the army major, she had sent an urgent telegram to Zaib.

It read, 'Please come and see me, something terrible has happened. I need you, please Zaib.'

Zaib had rushed there on the first flight she could catch. When she saw Devi she was shocked. She had lost what looked like at least a stone. Her eyes looked cold, different. She hugged Zaib and started crying, 'Oh Zaib, he has affairs.' Zaib felt her knees buckle.

As a dutiful wife Devi knew she had to try and forget Haider, as best she could, even thinking about him was a crime, a sin and a betrayal to her husband, so she decided to live as a dedicated wife, a loyal partner and in time a good mother, but within a few months of marrying him, Devika knew her parents had made a mistake. Her husband had an insatiable appetite for sex and he had mistresses all over the country. When he married Devi he was charming and loving and he knew how to seduce women. He couldn't stay with one woman for long though, no matter how beautiful or sought after she was, he hungered for the next, flirting outrageously in public and making overtures at them in front of his wife and friends. He enjoyed sexual challenges and many of the women he was seen with were wives of men in his batch from the army, and his friends. He enjoyed the betrayal.

In those first monsoon days of Devi's marriage, when she was still ignorant of her husband's philandering ways, she gave herself to him completely, not knowing what it was like to be touched sexually by a man or woman, she succumbed to him immediately. She moaned more loudly at his insistence when she had an orgasm, enjoying every moment of it. After the shock of his first affair, she thought his lovemaking had become more brutal, and his eyes deceived her every second he was inside her. She couldn't orgasm any more and of course he knew it, but it didn't seem to bother him, as long as she provided him with the illusion that she had reached a climax so that he could enjoy himself. Eventually she managed to separate, in her mind, his affairs from her relationship with him. She told Zaib it was the most viable solution, like a business interaction. But her words belied her as she became increasingly unhappy nurturing every new misery that her husband gave her.

Usually his affairs would not last long but once things became very serious and Devi thought she would lose him. The most glamorous of his mistresses was Zubaida, the wife of a senior minister in Pakistan. He was fifty, she was thirty years younger. The rumours about why she had married him were obvious, but her haughtiness was enough to scare men into believing she was not game for any relationship, she was untouchable. Devi's husband met her at the opening ceremony of a hotel. No one could understand how a man with his plain looks and manner could seduce a woman of her famous looks and her caliber in society, but within months he was seen taking her to the most beautiful holiday resorts in the northern areas of Pakistan. They became inseparable, and the entire army society was talking about them. Their indiscretions eventually became so dangerous that they started receiving death threats. Her husband was not only an important man in the government, he was also a powerful man; he owned land in hundreds of acres and entire villages were his. He usually operated outside the law like many other feudal lords and land owners and could have anyone picked up and killed at will. But the couple was undeterred.

Devi was washing the dishes one day when there was a knock on the door. Her husband was still not back after ten days in Murree. There was another knock on the door; she almost ran to open it, hoping it would be him. A man in a blue *shalwar kameez* and wrapped in a striped red and gold shawl stood in front of her.

'Where is the bastard, *behenchod*?'

'Who?'

'That *behenchod* husband of yours! You tell him next time he messes with other people's wives he will not live to tell the world. Understand!? I will come back for him!'

Devi was trembling for hours after he left.

When Haider came home that evening, Devi begged him to leave her. She said she didn't want to end up a widow. 'Please do it for the sake of the children if not for me.' A coward at heart and a realist too he knew those men meant business and he never saw Zubaida again but he became even more promiscuous than before. It was heard that Zubaida disappeared soon afterwards. One of the rumors was that she was sent to a village where her husband ordered his local villagers to rape her and drown her in the river. No one dared to investigate. The police were either paid off to keep quiet or threatened to do so. That was quite normally the routine in such cases.

The public humiliation only made him worse. He started picking up women from stale street corners and paying them for sex. He enjoyed paying for sex and then coming home to Devi. He told his friends it made him feel more alive and superior.

Over the years Devi had stopped asking him where he was going, but even then after all those years it was painful. She couldn't stand up to him and even if she had it would probably have made it worse for her. She was terrified that he might leave her, anything was better then that kind of degradation and society would have thrown her away and eaten her alive as they would her children.

She resumed her faith in God, this was her fate, the way it was meant to be. She prayed during the day. The nights were unforgiving, they told her she may be to blame, they told her she had lost and that she was a bad wife and mother. They told her such things over and over again so that the next day had failed her before it had even begun. She spent several hours thinking every night, lying in bed looking up at the ceiling, her moon eyes stripping the world of its beauty, every night, the last night of love.

ꕥ

9

Asad

Zaib breathed evenly. She hadn't moved for a while. What is that one thing that gives you faith, thought Alya, faith that can save you, faith that can kill you. She knew what her mother's faith was; she knew where her mother's God lived. Despite all that Devi had been through was still luckier? Did her *kind of faith* make a more content person? Couldn't she somehow instill a new faith in Zaib, a new faith that could save her? She thought about herself. She must have had faith to have survived Asad. But what kind of faith was that? It wasn't religious faith and it wasn't faith in herself. Then what was her faith based on? Her thoughts drifted again, back to Asad. Why me? Why did he choose me? After so much, she still wanted some sort of affirmation that Asad had actually loved her once, that that's why he did what he did all those years ago.

As a child Asad had always singled Alya out from the rest of his cousins, treating her as if she were special in some way. Zaib used to take the children home to Pakistan almost every summer for three months at a time, so the cousins met frequently. As children they had played games and she'd jumped on his back forcing him to give her a piggyback ride around the house. If she was naughty he would tickle her until she begged for forgiveness, '*na na na na* Asad bhai!!' she would squeal with excitement. He made sure she ate her vegetables and her fruit and he taught her boxing techniques in case someone 'tried to get fresh with her'. She had looked up to him as an older cousin who would protect her and shield her from the world if she needed him. She felt stronger when she was with him.

It was four years after Alya had shifted to Lahore that she heard the stories of events in Asad's life while she was away in Zakar. He was seen as good for nothing by most of their relatives because he refused to be tested on his intelligence. He told his teachers that he hated exams because he felt like a pig being fattened up for the slaughter. He often bunked classes and missed exams preferring to read books on philosophy and religion, deciphering his own meanings. The family's incessant taunts only made him more rigid and determined to follow his own beliefs. He ended up getting two A's and a B in his 'A' levels, but refused to study any further. Devi was devastated. 'What can I do, he is so bright. Oh God, where did I go wrong.' His father had long given up hope as far as Asad was concerned. He told Devi a day after Asad had made his important announcement, 'As far as I am concerned the boy can go to hell. I don't want to have anything to do with him!'

The day before that he had confronted Asad, 'Don't you dare even think about not going to university.'

'I don't want to be part of this system of education that moulds the way people think according to western ideals and capitalist beliefs!'

'You are young and idealistic. You have no idea what you are talking about. I'll ask you when you have to put food on the table for your wife and your children.'

'What makes you think I want to bring children into this decrepit world and frankly I am not sure I believe in the blissful sanctimony of marriage, after all look where it has got you and ammi.'

His father had replied with a resounding slap on his son's face, 'Don't you dare ever talk to me like that again.'

Asad had left the room with a disgusted expression on his face.

That year he turned eighteen. He moved out of home and started living with friends. Zaib tried to talk to him. 'Asad you are hurting everyone including your mother. What has she done to deserve this? At least live with them so your mother can see you.'

'Khala, you know her better than I. When was she there for me? Ammi has spent her entire life in bed. In fact I was meaning to ask you, did she ever walk?'

'Asad, don't be so cruel.'

'Khala please let me be the way I want to. You know how much I love you, but I don't think any of you can set the perfect example of how to live life even with your foreign degrees and your years of wisdom.'

Eventually Devi packed his things for him, 'I'll be here if you need me. Maybe one day you'll decide we are not all so stupid after all.'

'I know ammi, maybe I will, but that's for me to work out. I'll keep visiting when he's not around.'

With that he left.

*

'She was a beautiful girl. Slender, sensitive and warm, but there was something about her, something I could not put my finger on. I knew things weren't as they seemed right from the beginning.' That was what Devi had told Alya after the events of those few months.

Asad had met her at a wedding, where she was dancing to a Punjabi folk song. She was wearing a saffron *kurta* and white *churi daar* pajama with a six-metre *dupatta* wrapped around her delicate frame. As if dipped in turmeric, she glistened like a fish in clear water. He wished he were an artist so that he could capture the ambience of her surroundings and the ethereal movements of her supple body undulating to the rhythm of the song. She was mesmerizing. It was as if he could never actually touch her ethereal form. He was scared to approach her in case she rejected him, so he asked a friend to find out her phone number.

The next day he called her. She sounded shy on the phone. That perplexed him because it contradicted the confident woman he had seen the previous day, but it added a certain mystery to her personality and he became even more curious about her. She agreed to meet him for dinner. Face to face she was brimming with self-assurance. She didn't hide the fact that she was physically attracted to Asad. After dinner he took her to a local rest house where she shed her clothes easily and they quickly progressed to giving each other oral sex and then making love. Licking her everywhere, smelling her, fondling her taut breasts in his hands was the most sensual experience he had ever had. They started to meet every week, enjoying each other, sometimes making love at least two or three times in one day. She made him feel alive, wanted.

He decided to talk to Devi. 'Ammi, I really love her. She is special.'

'Asad, you are only nineteen. How will you support her and how can you be sure she is the one?'

'Ammi we will figure out a way. The most important thing is that I love her.'

Devi had let things run their course, thinking they would both eventually grow out of each other. 'They are just children,' she had said.

He planned his future with Irum with every new meeting. But Irum suffered from chronic asthma, and she started to disappear for days on end, unable to get out of bed. She told him he couldn't come to the house to see her as her father was strict. 'He has a really bad temper, so it's best if we just meet somewhere outside.'

He had his head on her bare stomach. They had just made love. 'Irum I want to marry you.'

Her eyes moistened, but they were expressionless. 'Thank you for loving me so much.' She sat up and started putting her clothes on mechanically, 'But I think your parents won't agree. For a start I am six years older than you and secondly, I am not exactly of your class, am I?'

'Oh I don't believe in all that shit, you know that. That's what I am running away from. I will marry you and no one can stop me. That's final.'

She smiled at him affectionately. The subject didn't come up again that day.

They had arranged to meet in a quiet motel where Asad had slipped a 500-rupee note to the receptionist. 'Make sure no one disturbs us.'

Irum arrived looking pale and drained. Asad was used to seeing small pricks in her arms from where the doctors had given her injections for her more severe asthma attacks, but today her arms were blue.

'What happened?'

'It was just a really bad attack and they couldn't find my veins because of the previous pricks.'

He was particularly loving that day, caressing her arms and kissing her all over. 'My love, I am so sorry you have to go through all of this.'

Over the next few months Asad felt her health was deteriorating rapidly and he became increasingly worried. He thought he should talk to her father about consulting another doctor.

'No Asad, my doctor is the best in the city for allergies and asthma, we've done our research, its no good. I just have to live with it. I will be alright, don't worry.'

'Ok, fine but I want to ask your father for your hand in marriage.'

She snapped at him, 'Asad this is not the right time besides I can't let you come to the house.'

'Why?'

'Because it's too embarrassing.'

'Why? You can tell me, believe me my family has plenty of embarrassing secrets, nothing shocks me anymore.'

'He is an alcoholic.'

There was a short pause and then he said, 'Okay, so? That's not so bad, it's an illness like any other and he needs help. Let me meet him, maybe I can help.'

'No Asad, please can we just leave it for now.'

He did for her sake. But on her birthday he decided to make an exception and surprise her. Surely she'd forgive him when she saw the five-dozen gladiolas in his hands and the diamond ring he had bought after begging his mother for the money, 'I promise I'll return every penny,' he had said to Devi. If she did love him as much as he loved her, he was convinced it was only a matter of time before they were married anyway.

He rang the doorbell of her house, but no one answered. After five minutes of waiting he heard a man's gruff voice, 'Who is it?'

'Is that uncle? Is Irum home?'

'No, no she is not home, now go away!'

'Can I meet uncle, I mean her father?'

'What father? He's been dead ten years.'

Shocked, he had no idea what was happening. Deciding to ignore the man, he walked over to the back of the house, and tried to peep through one of the bedroom windows. The curtain of one of the windows was slightly parted. There she was, a lifeless creature, his Irum on her bed, flat and grey, pale dead flesh, motionless, oblivious to the world. Everything looked hazy. What was she doing? What was going on?

'Irum!' he called with concern.

'Someone help!' A million things went through his mind, was she dead? Why was that man lying about her? Who was he? Maybe he was a mad man who had broken in and hurt her. He desperately tried to open the window. Luckily, the latch was loose and he opened it and climbed in. There she was, seemingly a motionless body on the bed.

The room was a garbage can of needles of all sizes. There was a strange medicinal smell mixed with the stink of vomit in the air. In the right hand corner of the room there was a blackish-brown liquid split on the floor and next to it a box of matches. Irum was sprawled on her bed, frail and lizard-like, and on closer inspection shaking gently, the last trails of some kind of fit still contorting her battered body. Time had stopped. A vaporous quietness sizzled the air. He picked her up in a daze and took her to a hospital where he knew one of the doctors.

'Please help her; I didn't want the police to find out so I brought her to you.'

'Who is she?'

'Just a friend.'

A week later she was told to go home. Asad tried to be as understanding as he could but she didn't talk about it much. All she said was, 'I was ashamed to tell anyone. People here talk and so I just lied.' She promised not to take drugs anymore and for a while she seemed better, looked healthier.

Things appeared to be getting back to normal. She and Asad met frequently and they never talked about that day, simply pretending it didn't happen. Asad tried to put things passed them taking one day at a time.

One morning the phone rang. It was Shehryar, an old friend.

'Yaar Asad, I have to see you, its really important.'

'What is it?'

He came over.

'Asad yaar please don't be upset, it's bad news.'

'Just get on with it, will you! And it better not be one of your silly pranks.'

'Ney, its Irum yaar,' he said hesitating.

'What's happened to Irum, you crazy son of a ...'

'Yaar Asad I am sorry, she's been seen with uncle.'

'Which uncle?'

'Uncle. Your father.'

'*Haram zada,* the bastard, I will kill you! How could you even say such a thing!'

He grabbed his collar and started punching him. The boy screamed, 'Please Asad, at least listen!!' Asad's eyes were bloodshot. 'I'll show you. He's been seen a few minutes ago.'

Shehryar took him to a restaurant where he saw his father having dinner with Irum. She was fawning over him, nodding and smiling while he spoke.

'They say he gives her money for her drugs. Some people have even seen her standing at street corners now. Asad I am sorry but you had to know.'

Asad spoke without emotion in a dead flat tone. 'The bastard. He knew I wanted to marry her.'

He went to his mother's cupboard, found two bottles of Valium, each containing 30 tablets, crushed them and mixed them in a glass of neat vodka: the blue powder folded in the vaporous streaked liquid and sank. He drank it quickly and climbed into bed after locking the door.

The last thing Asad remembered before falling asleep was the sky painted with pigeon blood, lonely trees littered with their bodies; red pigeons hanging over black boughs in a morbidly artistic twist of fate.

⁂

The blue swirled round and round and round. Zaib was still sleeping. Maybe when she wakes up I will give her a sleeping pill to keep her calm. What will I do then? Call Sonia. Maybe Devi khala …

The blue swirled round and round … … the blue drowning in white water …

⁂

Alya walks into Asad's room quietly. His room is lit up with two red lamps and all Alya can see is a deep red glow surrounding the bed and a few decorations he has kept as ornaments from various places he has been to. Again she thinks he might have read her thoughts of the last few days. It would be so embarrassing if he knew how I obsess about him, she thought. When she finally does look up at him, he is staring at her lips, not saying a word and she feels slightly uncomfortable. Her legs feel weak and she wants to speak, but nothing comes out. Before she can formulate anything properly in her mind, he picks her up and places her gently on his bed. She feels a rush of excitement in her stomach and is strangely ashamed of what is happening to her body despite herself. First he kisses her gently on the lips, then he slowly unties the chord of his shalwar; his movements are measured. Without taking off his *shalwar* he slides her hand inside it and places his erect penis in her hand. She wants to but cannot move. A feeling of nausea tickles her throat. But she is still so conscious of what he would think of her if she tries to draw back that she controls herself and follows his guiding hands believing that for this too he must have a good reason, something that is beyond her understanding. He starts to kiss her over and over again on her lips and makes her stroke his penis, gently at first and gradually harder and with more friction. She has no idea what is happening – exactly – but she thinks if this goes on his skin will soon peel off. She dares not speak but carries on. Her hand hurts. Finally she hears a soft moan coming from his lips and feels a fountain of thick, warm, gluey liquid burst all over her hand. He removes her hand and cleans it and himself up with a towel, calmly. Then he says, 'Oh sweetheart you are so wonderful, I love you.' He smiles at her affectionately and then kisses her again. 'Good night my love, you better go to your room now, before someone wakes up. I always knew you were special, the only woman who could be mine.' She is sweating, her heart thumping and she can't really understand the last few words he said. She tiptoes into her room feeling exhausted. There, in the dark with Sonia sleeping soundly next to her, she cannot contain herself and bursts out crying and laughing at the same time, rocking backwards and forwards until her stomach hurts and tears roll down her cheeks. And then she says to herself in a whisper, 'He loves me. He said he loves me!'

☙❧

10

Ladybird

Zaib had been looking for her everywhere. The servant's quarter was locked; she wasn't in the garden or in any of the rooms in the house.

'Ghazala!'

She sat down on the grass, out of breath and tired. Suddenly, Ghazala popped out from behind the house.

'Ghazala, where were you?'

'I was here all along Zaib, you just didn't look hard enough.' She had a wicked twinkle in her eye, but she was flustered and red. She laughed, running towards Zaib; she made tickling gestures towards her.

Zaib remained serious. 'What's wrong with your face?'

'I was running, silly girl!'

The next day Ghazala was lost again. Zaib even looked on the roof this time. Then she suddenly remembered there was one place she hadn't looked this time, there was a small extra room hidden behind the servant's quarter. No one ever went there. So she ran outside and rushed towards the room. As she got closer she heard noises coming from inside, strange noises like shuffling and scratching, she thought of cats and their babies in the dark. She thought of Ganga Ram hospital.

She knocked, 'Can I come in? Ghazala are you there?'

She heard her steady voice. 'Zaib I am coming.'

'What are you doing in there?'

A few moments later Ghazala came out looking hot and flustered.

'I was washing something ... Oh Zaib, can't you just leave me alone for now. I have other things to do too. I am not rich like you, I have to work to live, you know!' She cut through her.

'Fine, I'll just go back home. You come when you are ready.'

Zaib found her the next day in the quarter; she was singing and sweeping the floor.

'Why didn't you tell me Ghazala?'

'Tell you what?'

Could she have made a mistake? Was there someone in that room with Ghazala? Did she see someone climb out of the window or had she imagined it ... the convent children cut the sky with kites, the flat sky, and shredded it to its core, the sad sad sky...

'We were just children then, Ghazala and me, children who knew only about dreams... ' Zaib's eyes were full of tears, 'my poor poor Ghazala.' It was *him,* the talcum powder man, the gardener, who Zaib had played with as a child, Ghazala's stepfather who was with her. It was him. I remember now, I remember his body his head his arms. How could it be him? Somehow Zaib had blanked out what she saw that day, but it came back to her, later, with such clarity and she saw it all again and again... like a parasite film.

Ghazala was on her knees, while her stepfather, who was facing her, held her head with both hands. She could see Ghazala's head being pushed backwards and forwards like a doll's until finally he pushed her onto a *charpoy* lying in one corner of the room. He quickly pulled her *shalwar* down and lay down on top of her and then all Zaib could see was him moving up and down on top of Ghazala and at the time she thought he might squash her if he kept doing it. But Zaib could sense that something terrible had just happened. She did not understand it fully until Ghazala was gone, until it was too late. 'She couldn't have turned to anyone, she must have been so scared Devi.' She had sobbed all night talking about Ghazala to Devi, a few years after Devi's marriage.

The word was *dead.* That day when they had arrived from Nathia Gali Zaib knew something horrible had happened as soon as she had looked at her mother. Ghazala is dead. The word was dead, dead, dead. The finality of that word would have been kinder than what mummy had said – *she is with God now.* How could God be so cruel as to take Ghazala away from her forever? What kind of God was that? Her image of God had changed from that day on. God was not the kind, loving figure that she had prayed to, that could solve her pain, her anguish. God was someone who had caused her pain and suffering, someone who had taken her Ghazala away from her.

'She should have just said she was dead. I would have had more respect for her. But she betrayed me once again,' she had once told Alya.

'How did she die?' she had asked her mother.

Zaib had looked distant, 'Mummy told me she got hepatitis, but somehow I know if I were there she wouldn't have died. I would have done something.'

Mummy was always on a mission to make her daughters tough. When Zaib complained of period pain, she had said, 'Walk up and down and don't make a sound, the less noise you make the quicker you'll feel better.' Zaib had gone to her room and writhed in bed, trying to muffle her cries in her pillow so mummy couldn't see that she was *weak*. When Zaib got flu, she told her everyone got flu and that she had to just live through until she got better. 'Don't fuss Zaib,' she'd say, 'it's just a flu, you'll survive. Just don't drink cold water and stay warm.' The most she'd do is make sure she was clothed warmly, but sympathy was one thing she could rarely expect from mummy.

One day Zaib asked Devi, 'Do you think she'd care if I got cancer or some other really serious disease?' Devi had smiled affectionately and said, 'Zaib, she only does it to make you stronger, so that you can handle things bravely when you are older.' Zaib could not articulate her feelings in words, but she was sure what her mother was doing was definitely not making her stronger; in taking away a mother's warmth from her child it was in fact making her much weaker. Decades later she told Sonia how difficult it was to live up to 'mummy's expectations'. 'Every time I'd fail at something I'd feel I have to be brave and I wouldn't cry. For a long time I built a wall around me, and no one could get through, that was until I met Hassan. And how come she was so different with daddy anyway?'

Mummy... loving her, discarding her, re-inventing her, trying to make her as she wanted her to be, as if she were a model being moulded out of clay. Why was mummy always so adamant to make her pretty, presentable, polite? She had to dress in pink and white, wear white shoes, visit mummy's pathetic sisters and sit and listen to their endless advice for hours. Young as she was she knew they were just trying to make themselves feel better by putting her down just because she was Shafi's daughter who was successful and well known in the community –whereas they were married to nobodys, which did not matter to Zaib but for them it was everything. Then of course there was the constant war over Ghazala, a poor man's daughter; it was a war on all fronts.

Devi had asked Zaib once, 'Did you love her more than me?'

'Who?'

'You know, that girl, who always wore that shiny blue *shalwar kameez* people tell me about.'

'Devi, it was silk and she always wore it because I gave it to her. And by the way she had a name.'

'Well, did you?'

'I love you in a different way.'

Devi had just returned from Oxford and she said she was getting bored so their father found her a job at a local law firm as an office assistant. That was before she had met Haider. One morning she was in her room dressing up for work, when mummy came in, visibly shaken.

'What's wrong, are you alright?'

'Oh Devi, I have failed so badly. I tried to do everything for her.'

She sat on the bed holding on to Devi's arm. Devi took her hand.

'I have no patience anymore Devi, you weren't here and I had no one to tell.' She paused. 'Zaib was outside with that servant girl.'

Devi gave the name. 'You mean Ghazala.'

'They were doing something.'

Devi's feet felt cold.

'What were they doing?' She wasn't sure if she wanted to hear any more.

'I couldn't see anything properly, but I know something was going on.'

Devi lied, 'Mummy I am sure it was nothing, you must have been mistaken.'

Devi didn't know who to turn to, what to say, but she knew her mother was tired, tired of what was happening, tired of watching the people she loved, fall like dominoes. Unlike Zaib she tended to have more sympathy for her mother. She saw her as someone who had to be infallible to keep the family together, to seem to be made of iron even in the most difficult times because she *had to*. She wanted to help her but she didn't know how.

'She's acting up again. I don't know what else to do. Devi, I am going to send her away.'

'It won't solve anything. Anyway where will you send her? Why don't you try and talk to her. What about daddy?'

'Are you mad? He'll die! We can't tell him anything.'

As far as Devi was concerned, what she was trying to do was to give Zaib a tougher skin, to equip her for the world ahead, the world that was so much more unforgiving than a mother or father can ever be. But she knew it was also true that mummy was too involved with the lives of her sisters. She knew her mother felt responsible for her sisters' welfare since their parents had died when they were children. Mummy was always willing to turn a blind eye to anything her sisters said. Once Devi had asked her why. 'You know your *nani* died when I was only ten and they were even younger. They are like my children. I practically brought them up, plus you girls are privileged, you don't know what's it's like to grow up without a mother.' That was true but it was hardly something they should have had to pay the price for. Even so Devi had tried to defend her mother to Zaib more than once, 'Zaib, try and see it from her eyes, they are her children just like us. When they advise us or scold us she sees it as normal, as loving aunts scolding their nieces, she is blind as far as they are concerned.' Zaib had replied sarcastically, 'Well she shouldn't have given birth to us then – I mean if she already had children.'

Zaib was sent to boarding school soon after her mother had seen her with Ghazala in her quarter on her birthday. When she came back after three months for a holiday, she was stick thin and her hair looked like straw. She was supposed to go back but her father had taken a strong stand this time.

He looked down at the floor, rubbing his forehead with his fingers. 'We must keep her with us now. What has happened to her, she doesn't say a word! And now that she is here, tell your damn sisters to leave us alone, they are responsible for this, much more than any damn convent or boarding school!'

'Oh, you are so pathetic. Trust you to use them as scapegoats whenever it's convenient.'

Zaib was listening. She felt guilty, but when she went to sleep she was happy just to be back in her own bed. Two days later Ruksana, one of her khalas came to see her.

'Oh look who's back. So soon!'

Mummy gave her a severe look, 'That's enough Ruksana.'

A week later they had arrived after hearing about Zaib's stepsister, 'Oh my God what a tragedy, what a terrible terrible tragedy! Oh our poor Shafi, how is he holding up?' *Our Shafi.* 'And Zaib, what are you doing dressed in red, don't you know this is a somber occasion.' Mummy had just sat there quiet and expressionless. You bitches, thought Zaib, you are just here to gloat. When she ran to daddy's room to protect him from them, he told her to let them be, he told her it was alright, he always told her it was alright when it really wasn't. He told her that even if he was falling apart himself like on that particular day. Earlier that day mummy was marching up and down waiting for the driver to get home from dropping daddy to work.

Zaib wanted to visit a school friend, 'Mummy, can I go to Ayesha's?'

'No, I have to go shopping, not today.'

'Oh please mummy.'

'I said no Zaib, and that's final.'

When mummy came home four hours later, she was falling over with all sorts of things, clothes, sheets, flowers, and utensils for the kitchen....

'Come here *beta*.'

Oh my God, what was it this time, another lacy frock. She wanted to shut her eyes tightly and wish mummy would disappear before her next move.

'Look at this, do you like it?' Her mother handed it over to her smiling confidently. It was a silk dress with pink lace on the sleeves and collar. Oh God, I knew it.

'Isn't it beautiful?'

'It has too much lace. Why can't I choose myself?'

'Because you are too young and obviously too insolent as well.'

After work daddy had planned to go and visit his 'other children', Zaib's stepbrother and sisters. She always felt happy for him when he went to see them because mummy hardly ever allowed him to go. Today he had been gone a long time and Zaib was anxious. She knew his eldest daughter was full term pregnant but she wasn't due till the following week. There had also been some talk about complications; the doctors said she had high blood pressure. She was too young to understand the details besides daddy didn't talk much about them to Zaib or Devi. Finally the front door opened.

As soon as Zaib heard the sound of her father's footsteps she knew something was wrong.

'Daddy?'

She looked at him. His eyes looked grey and seemed to have aged within hours, his lips were dry.

'Zaib go to your room.'

He went into his room and shut the door. Her mother went after him.

When she returned, she looked drained. Something was obviously terribly wrong. 'Mummy will you do something?' She looked at her reassuringly but didn't answer. Mummy would take care of him, everything would be all right. Mummy was good with misery, besides she was strong and invincible. Zaib had felt safe in the knowledge that mummy would take care of things.

'It's going to be tough now Zaib, his daughter died. She died in childbirth this afternoon. You should be with him right now.'

His daughter, my sister. Mummy was Diana, the Goddess of War, yet her eyes gave her away. Zaib was looking for an answer, a way of consoling her father, her dear dear father, but she couldn't focus on anything. The baby came to her mind and the vague outline of a dead sister she had not known.

'Did the baby survive?'

'Yes.'

Zaib went to her father. He was on the bed staring at the ceiling.

'Daddy I am sure she is in heaven with God.'

He gave a deep sigh, 'Yes Zaib she is, she is...'

'I will pray for her. Can I go and see the baby some time?'

'Yes, I'll take you in a few days.'

She sat next to him on his bed for several minutes holding his hand while he continued to look up at the ceiling, his eyes a glazed grey myriad of emotion.

That night she cried as she thought of how much pain her father must be in. The next morning as she sat still on the beige couch of her mother's crystal room, she thought of ways to make her father feel better. Suddenly Ghazala came to her mind. Ghazala would be waiting for her outside and she had started feeling a strange sensation in her stomach every time she thought of Ghazala. It was so powerful she couldn't understand it until that day on her birthday in Ghazala's quarter. All her life she remembered it as being the best feeling in the world.

Mummy was rushing in and out of rooms looking worried and screaming at the servants. The servants were preparing for guests to arrive to say *duah* for Zaib's dead half-sister. They were spreading white sheets all over the carpets. Ghazala was outside. Zaib was counting the flowers on the beige couch. It was an exquisite couch, soft and cotton wool-like, bright as daylight in winter. Zaib brushed her hand across it just to feel the flowers on her hands. Their unreality and the softness of the couch comforted her. When the clock struck nine, mother told her to go to her room and wear something more presentable. 'You are looking like a Christmas tree, Zaib, with this huge *gotey ka dupatta* and red lipstick.'

She went to her room and looked at herself in the mirror. She was wearing her mother's red lipstick and her eyes were black with kohl. She had wrapped a red *dupatta* (with *gota* on the edges) around herself and she was sparkling with imitation jewellery. That morning she had been acting in a play she had invented in her room, with Ralph. She was a dancing girl this time, trying to please the great nawab in his haveli. She danced and danced until she fell at his feet (just like in an Indian movie, *Pakeezah*, she had seen recently) and he finally picked her up and chose her to be his wife. She was dressing in her bridal clothes to marry him when mummy interrupted her. She said Zaib had to help in the kitchen. Zaib was still thinking about her nawab and in these clothes she felt she was still there in his haveli with him. Now mummy wanted her to change her clothes and break the dream. It wasn't fair but she knew she had to go, so she was forced to wear a cream *shalwar kameez* and wash the make up off her face. But there was one thing she just had to do and that was to see Ghazala before the guests arrived.

Outside the sky was grey. Ghazala was chasing a chicken. The chicken was bouncing up and down and Ghazala had a stick in her hand. Zaib stopped her.

'Ghazala, why are you upsetting the chicken?'

'Don't be silly Zaib, it's just a chicken.'

'It has feelings too.'

'Zaib we eat chickens, remember?'

'Well, that's different.'

She left the chicken and they decided to try and find ladybirds in the garden instead. It was usually in rainy weather that ladybirds appeared and Zaib loved to watch them climb tiny leaves and blades of grass with their little spindly legs and spotty backs.

'Look Zaib, look at the way they crawl through grass, for them the blades of grass are like big trees and when they climb over the bumps on leaves it must be like climbing mountains.'

Zaib looked at them, fascinated by their strength and persistence to get somewhere. She marveled at their perfection, the faultless symmetry of their bodies and the vibrant red that was brighter than any red rose she had ever seen. She had carried them in her hands many times before but today she took one with her in the house. 'I will talk to her when the guests are here. We will have our own secrets,' she thought.

'Zaib don't, she won't like it indoors, her home is here, outside!' But Zaib had already gone.

Inside, she gently placed the ladybird on the sofa. Zaib watched her make her way across the sofa patiently and systematically. Zaib lifted her when she thought she might be tired of one place and decided to take her to the bedroom. The ladybird needed a new adventure too. On the way, she suddenly stretched her legs and two big black monstrous wings sprouted from the sides of her body! Zaib let out a scream of absolute terror. Her mother came running into the hallway. 'What is wrong Zaib?' Her heart was thumping. The ladybird was flying across the room, but mummy couldn't see it. 'Zaib, what is it?'

'Mama something happened to the ladybird.'

'Oh, for God's sake Zaib. What a fuss, I got the scare of my life.'

Zaib's heart was still racing. She ran into her father's room. He wasn't there. She could hear the water running in the bathroom. 'Daddy, I have to ask you something!'

'Zaib I am coming, I'm almost finished.'

She waited on his bed. He came out with his towel wrapped around his waist.

'Daddy, what is wrong with ladybirds?'

'Nothing. What do you mean?'

'Daddy, the ladybird grew wings while I was holding her.'

He squeezed a smile. 'Zaib all ladybirds have wings.'

She realized it was her who hadn't seen one fly before. They had always flown; as long as ladybirds had existed they had been able to fly. She just didn't know it. She felt cheated and angry. She remained thoughtful for a long time, ladybirds proliferating all over the room, their cunning black eyes bulging; they flew towards her, mockingly. They grew to monstrous proportions climbing all over her, ready to devour her. The huge matrix of thin black tentacles and spidery extensions engulfed her, until she was gasping for breath.

'Zaib are you alright honey?' It was auntie Tasneem, her mother's friend from work. She was a doctor too. Zaib could smell the methylated spirit from her hands. One of the ladybirds was choking her. 'Zaib?'

'I am fine, thank you auntie.' She liked this auntie but auntie's perfect face was about to fragment. 'Auntie I have to go to the toilet.'

She ran outside to tell Ghazala what had happened. Ghazala hugged her.

'Zaib, they can't do anything to us; the trees will protect us. From now onwards ladybirds are our enemies. We will never play with them again.'

ᴕ

11

Centipede Land

Alya wondered how Zaib had grown so frail, so alone. Zaib referred to Hassan only as 'daddy' now and clung to him when she was around, asking him to cradle her in his arms. Alya found it revolting, pitiful, disappointing. All those years ago in Zakar, ammi had had hopes and aspirations, a chance to finally live her life without the shackles of her mother's expectations or her father's devotion. Now she was in a new place, perhaps an unfamiliar one, but that could not have been the only factor.

Was it inevitable? Or had the breakdown begun long before that ... when Zaib had others.... Ralph.... the matchstickmen and her childhood fears and dreams.

Two days after arriving in Zakar, Hassan joined a US-based oil company. Busy in his new job he was usually out the entire day. 'It was one of the most difficult periods of my life,' Zaib later told Devi. 'I thought I'd die waiting for him.'

In the morning she stayed in bed until she could no longer bear to think with her eyes closed. She was so used to spending her days in her father's garden she craved to be outdoors. She would open the front door and walk outside. But the grey cement floor was too hot to stand on and the air was humid. It was difficult even to breathe. On one such day when Hassan came back home, she sobbed into his arms, 'Oh Hassan, it was miserable without you today.'

'Give it time, we'll make friends, plus on the weekend we'll check out what there is to do in the city and I'll hire a driver for you so you can look around.'

But that took time and meanwhile, the desolation of her days suffocated her. One day rolled into the next and she would spend hours reading mindless magazines or watching television. She watched the minute hand on the clock chase her and waited for Hassan impatiently. Usually at about 7 pm she would put on her lipstick and sit down in the sitting room straining to hear the faintest sound of his car pull up. When he finally came in she would run up to him and kiss him. Then she would sit on his knee, absorbed in his words while he told her of the days' events. He sometimes looked at her with the warm amusement one looks at a child with.

'Hassan, you will never get tired of me, will you?'

'Can anyone ever get tired of such a crazy girl?'

Four months passed by. She started to look for clues on the streets and in shops about how her city was without her. But more than the days, the nights were restless. She was on the inside looking out, unable to break into the world and strapped to her nightmares.

Hassan tried to console her. 'Zaib, why don't you catch a cab and go around the city a bit? I'll take you to the British Council Library on the weekend. Why don't you start reading again?'

So she did. She started reading – she reread Austen, she reread Hardy, she reread Camus, she reread Sartre. For some reason new books and new writers didn't interest her. Perhaps it was because the books she had read and their stories took her back to a certain time in her childhood, especially the times she had spent discussing them with Devi. She read them, smelt them, believed them again and again and finally she regained the courage to revisit her old files of poems, poems she had written as a teenager.

One day she told Hassan, 'You know, as a child I would dream of becoming a writer. I have written some poems that I want to try and get published now.'

He encouraged her with trepidation. She showed him some of them.

'Do you like them?' she asked nervously.

'They are very otherworldly, just like my Zaib. I am sure you can get published,' he said after reading them with interest.

'You don't like them, I can tell.'

'Of course I do, but I am not a literature person, so I might not be the best person to ask.'

She decided to send them to publishers in England and the US anyway. 'Oh Hassan if I get published I'll be so happy!'

Her first response read,

Dear Ms Hassan,

I received your short collection of poems, which I read with interest. I particularly liked the tone and unusual style of "The Letter". However, at the present time we do not think the poems are suitable for the coming edition of....

I wish you the best of luck elsewhere.

Yours sincerely,

John Wren

'What he means is he thought they were useless!!'

That night, Zaib cried for hours. Hassan held her in his arms. A few more letters of rejection arrived and she became so disheartened that she decided to give up. No amount of love or consoling could make her feel better. She would lash out at Hassan at the slightest provocation. One day when he came back from work she told him she wanted to go out for dinner.

'Zaib I am tired, can we please do it tomorrow, I've had a long day.'

'You are just so selfish. You and your damn office, that's all that matters. That damn damn office! You don't care about me!'

And it continued... one day and the next, the hate, the love and the regret that comes with hurting those you love the most. The last thing Hassan was, was selfish, she knew that. But there was no faith in herself. How could she have faith in him? She was a failed writer, a failed person, a bad wife and mother.

Most days she lived in that indeterminate time of day when it is neither day or night, when the sky is dusty with the dim anticipation of night and the day is fading. One day at lunch she sat alone savouring the smell of hot food on her plate, she watched the smoke tails rise from her plate and follow the memories of her husband and her picking flowers with each other in the many gardens and meadows they had visited together. She followed the twitter of ghosts. She saw

Hansel and Gretel, her big daddy prince, her Hassan, *who she now called daddy out of love,* and her on a huge water lily sailing afar to the Eastern horizon where Arabian Knights save their princesses from evil men; she saw a journey to a small hut in which an old man sat eating his soup huddled in front of a hearth telling her and Hassan fables of long ago, of gnomes and dwarfs and fairies saving people and creating darkness and light all at the same time. That day she ate her lunch slowly, languidly. She tried to read a new book at the same time and wondered how someone who writes so badly could get published and yet she couldn't and she thought about Ralph and his pointy chin. After lunch she was sure she heard the doorbell and went to check at the door. It was the newspaperman. She took the paper from him and glanced at the front page. All she saw was the date on the right hand corner, the rest were just black scribbles.

On her way back inside the porch she sees a striped yellow and black creature, possibly a centipede but she isn't sure. She is struck by 'his' rare beauty, his perfect build and his precise movements, but is also terrified that he will follow her into the house. She runs inside and brings back a small bucket of water. She starts to splash it on him frantically, weakly. The memory of a water fight with her father makes her shudder. She throws water on him about a dozen times until part of his body breaks away from the rest and he lies still. She sighs; it was over. It seems hours before she can walk away. She stands looking at it thoughtfully. Spineless, floppy men follow her in to the house of swollen furniture. She returns outside after a couple of minutes to make sure the creature is dead, but it is no longer there. She tries to find it. She is stunned. It stares back at her with defiance and bitterness, sweet ice on its translucent skin. Slowly she approaches it while it glides across a tile. She screams for help, but no one hears her. He is alive, alive, but broken. She feels a knife in her chest. He looks shorter, twisted. The matchstickmen climb up her legs. She combs the area for something, anything to pick it up with, and finds a dead leaf. She lifts the creature onto the leaf with weak hands. Her legs are shaking. She walks across the porch to the gate, opens it and quickly drops the leaf outside. She cannot bear the creature anymore. She runs back in. Things in the house looked different after that, distorted and distant. She had opened the door to centipede land.

ఌ

Although Devi and Zaib were writing to each other regularly, it became more and more difficult for Zaib to stay away from Devi for long periods of time, and she frequently visited her in Lahore. She and Hassan had started talking less at dinner though they often wondered what the other was thinking. One night as she lay beside him she thought of Larkin's poem "Taking in Bed" and the lines resonated in her head over and over, "Dark towns heap up on the horizon…. At this unique distance from isolation it becomes still more difficult to find words at once true and kind, or not untrue and not unkind". Her need for him was growing and so was her love, yet the loneliness multiplied everyday heavy on her chest like dead air. One morning she woke up in a submarine looking out of an oval window at rainbow-coloured fish and felt she had been buried alive. But then there were days when Hassan would cover her feet with a blanket in the winter, just before leaving for work on tiptoes.

Devi wrote to her again, five months after the last letter.

Zaib

I am sorry it is always so long between letters. It has been so hectic with the boys at school. Asad has been missing classes and his teacher called me to the office. It was so embarrassing. It's all because of their father you know. He is never home. I can't discipline them on my own. I feel so powerless sometimes. But then sometimes he is good to us. We are well provided for and he is never nasty to me. Well, that's life. It's all written for us Zaib. (Yes, thought Zaib, it is all written, all pre-ordained, all decided, as if we were vegetables, or worse still animals for the slaughter, caged, impotent.) How are you both? The desert is very exotic; you must make the most of it! Come and visit when you get the chance, both of you. I will write again soon. In the meantime don't forget it is my husband's birthday on the 3rd of next month, don't forget to send him a card.

I love you. Look after yourself,

Devi

Devi's face looked sad. A sad face of acceptance. She killed her over and over again in her mind.

'Daddy, she is so subservient to that monster, she even wants us to send him a birthday card!'

'Zaib, we all are weak in one way or another. Just don't send the card.'

But she could detect the signs of misery in Devi's letter because she knew her sister, she knew her sister like she knew her father's mango trees, every tremor, every ache, every new beginning. She told Hassan she had to go to her immediately. As she was leaving for the airport she looked back at him. 'Never stop loving me.'

He hugged her, 'Zaib, I will always love you. Just come back soon ok?'

And he did. He always loved her.

❧

During that trip Zaib made a visit to her mother's grave. She had only visited her mother's grave once before. On that occasion she didn't cry or feel the need to mourn, she just felt as if a centipede was shifting and gnawing inside her and waking up the freezing grey stones around her.

Mummy's gravestone was damaged too (she noticed that the second time). The first time she visited the gravestone she didn't associate it with her mother at all. She stared at the overgrown grass surrounding it and imagined pixie-faced boys and girls making circles around it, hand in hand and fairies looking after mummy inside the ground with mud balls in their hands and brown chocolate dribbling from their cunning little mouths and hands. Then she looked at the precarious gravestone closely and read it over and over again. Something was wrong; she thought about how each word must have been carelessly etched into the stone by a stranger. There was something incomprehensible about it. How could someone write anything about *her* mother? 'Here lies... wife of ... died 19...' She repeated the words in her mind over and over again, 'died 1955...' When ... when? What about where, how and the rest? Was there no more to say about mummy? The stranger lingered in Zaib's mind so that she could give *him* a face and thin, mean hands like Ralph's. She hated him more when she looked into his dishonest paper eyes and if he were there she would have bludgeoned his head to bits with mummy's gravestone. .... She was sure she shouldn't be here. She kept repeating the words to herself, but she couldn't find her voice. 'Our beloved son... died on...' 'Attaullah Khan, son of... died in...' "Margaret... 1921 to 1950 died tragically.' The last one grew inside her imposing itself on her like a virus, for some reason she imagined Margaret must have been the victim of a car accident because she was only twenty-nine when she died. She felt nauseous; she suddenly knew she hadn't been given a choice about the growing dead around her or the words written about them. The dead were murmuring something under Zaib's feet while the living were looking up towards the sky ready for their inevitable retreat ... Zaib saw a man walking across the graveyard. Whose grave had he been visiting, she wondered? She wished she could touch him, just once! He disappeared but her eyes followed his trail for a long time afterwards and the longing didn't end. Looking at the spot where he had left his mark, she thought about her own future. What about the rest of her life? Her small life looked pitiful already, 'Zaib, wife and daughter of...' What more could anyone say about her? The words were being churned out, one by one, the fat B's and the cunning i's, the vicious e's and the maddening o's. They were going to rotate endlessly with or without her consent. She threw them away before abandoning mummy and her grave; it was a final effort at giving life a meaning but as she walked away, she realized she had lost the battle to save herself.

☙❧

12

Daddy

She arched her back with pleasure. Her mouth open like a child's waiting for its next mouthful. He brought his mouth close to hers and let his saliva drop onto her tongue slowly without touching her lips. It was as if she was one breath away from death and a little closer to life. His hand covered her mouth as she started to orgasm. He pushed deeper, more intensely and she shut her eyes tight. An hour later Zaib was curled up in his arms, fast asleep.

Outside, the sun was burning holes in fruit. Zaib crushed a grape between her teeth. She looked up at the cracking leaves of an old palm tree, veins breaking the stone blue sky. The sound of crashing glass startled her; a boy had kicked an empty coke bottle across the road into a dustbin. A lizard had her pinned to the footpath with its charcoal eyes, mocking tongue. She recalled the last time she had killed a lizard. Centipedes crawled all over the pavement. She could hear the constant sound of church bells in the distance and began to feel desperate to get to the church. She pulled herself away from the boy, the lizard, the heat and walked in short quick steps following the trail of the church bells. On the way ants scurried across the sun-fractured earth, a footstep away from death. A man in a Mercedes pulled over and rolled his window down, 'A beautiful woman like you should not be so lonely like this, come for a ride with me, come on darling!' She saw his wet lips on her breasts and felt sick. He shrugged his shoulders and drove off. She had the smell of fish in her nostrils from the day before. Fish behind glass, past street vendors shining with sweat and lanes of leaking dust light. She had to find the church. The second turning had come and the chimes were louder but she still couldn't see the church. Her breathing became uneven and she was suffocating. 'Mama, mama. Where is the church?' A woman in white took her hand, she had big pink lips, 'Zaib, you need sugar.' 'I hate sugar, please don't make me....' Her chest tightened. 'Sugar is good for you.' 'I think her blood pressure is falling.' 'Take her to the other room.' 'She has always been sickly.' 'She hasn't eaten for days.' 'Is she very ill?' 'She looks like a rake.' 'Have you thought about a psychiatrist?' 'She is sick.'

'Zaib, wake up it's only a dream, Zaib Zaib Zaib Zaib it's me, daddy, open your eyes.' 'Dada you are back, where were you? The church is too far away I tried to...' She had eggshell feet.

'Zaib, wake up it's me, Hassan.' She woke up with sweat trickling down her temples...

'Hassan where is the church? I have to find the church.'

Alya was getting nervous as the hours passed. Any minute now her mother would wake up. What would she be like this time? Would she be a new version of Zaib or would she be a re-invented version of one of the older ones? It suddenly occurred to her that she might be the sanest of them all. We all have versions, we just don't act them out. She did. But was she really that brave if it wasn't in her control? She remembered Zaib telling her as a child, 'Alya remember one thing, most things are in your hands and you can change them if you want to. If you feel they are not, you are probably just kidding yourself.' That was after Alya had just about scraped through her 'O' level exams. Was that in her control? But Devi khala looked at things differently, she believed in fate, that's why she had spent most of her life in bed, thinking her life just could not have been any other way. The only way to deal with it was to either be sick or to spend it in bed trying to make others feel sorry for you. That was one way of dealing with life. The other way was of course waking up to your versions, accepting them and being true to each one. That was Zaib's way.

Alya thought of her own ... the life that she had lived was a gift from so many people, especially the two most important men in her life, her father and Asad. She thought of where Asad was now ... abandoned by his wife, his children.... Was that punishment enough for what he had done to her; was it enough or would it be worse if she told him after all these years she still loved him. That would be the coup de grace and maybe that would finally finish him off. But was that what she really wanted? Did she want him in some particular place or was this enough?

The first time Asad had had sex with her was five days after she had his 'stuff' all over her hands that night she and Sonia were staying at Devi khala's house and she had sneaked out of her room and into his. Zaib and Hassan had left for the US for a two-month vacation. Asad had called her into his room late at night.

She remembered it all so clearly – the days, the nights, the face of each morning, each night – at least how it all began. After telling her how special she was he had slowly started taking off her clothes and kissing her all over her neck. Her legs felt were weak and she could hear her heart in her chest. She wanted to cry, laugh, hide, but she was too embarrassed to express anything in particular. Gradually, he took off all her clothes and started to stroke her small, hard tender breasts. He slipped one hand between her thighs and stroked her vagina with his fingers. 'You are nice and wet my darling.' Then he gently placed his hand on her mouth and quickly put his penis inside her. She tried to scream but his hand muffled her cries. 'Shh shhh ... it'll be over soon and then you'll enjoy it ... good girl, good girl ...' The agony, agony. *Let me go please please, let me go. It's hurting, please.* '"Go and wash up.' She could hardly move. A trickle of dark red blood slid down her right thigh. Eventually, she managed to get up and walk over to the bathroom. When she came back he smiled at her. 'Are you alright *jaano*?' The world was blurred as tears filled her eyes, but she was silent. Silent and ashamed. She sat in front of him with her legs tightly squeezed together. He opened a new packet of cigarettes and took one out.

It has been two months and Alya and Asad have sex regularly. She usually wants to cry after sex. She is not sure why because she enjoys it, mostly. She waits for her periods anxiously every month because Asad is scared she might be pregnant every time she is late. Her breasts are hard and they hurt. Today he is buckling his belt quickly. Devi has gone out to a dinner with her husband, who is in Lahore. The servants are in their quarters. The phone rings. Zaib and Hassan are still on their honeymoon holiday, trying to resolve matters.

'It's Zaib Khala.'

Alya runs to the phone, almost tripping on the way.

'Ammi, where are you?' she says in a small voice.

'Ammi please come home soon, I am missing you so much?'

Zaib says something to her quickly. The conversation is short and she puts the phone down abruptly and comes back into the room where Asad is waiting for her. He smiles affectionately. 'They'll be home soon, don't look so worried.' He suggests they go for a drive to cheer her up. She wraps a dupatta *around her head so that not even one hair is visible. 'It is written clearly that women are too precious to be looked at by other men. You are like our jewellery. Now you wouldn't put your jewellery out on the street for thieves to come and steal it, would you? The same is true for a woman, she is to be protected and nurtured, hidden from the prying eyes of other men.' He is the puppet of his concepts, his baseless ideals. She knows that somewhere inside her. Sheets of rain chase them. Although it is six o'clock the light hasn't faded outside, she is looking for her mother on the streets.*

'Alya, what are you looking at?'

'The rain.'

'No, you weren't. I saw you looking at him.'

'Who?'

'Don't act so innocent Alya! That man walking on the pavement!'

His features are contorted and he is shaking with rage. She can see vile thoughts in his head and murder in his eyes. This happens almost everyday now, but she doesn't resist him. His neurosis is crippling her, breaking her down, second by second. She is groping in her child's head to think of the reasons necessary to live. He is saying she is selling herself to men because she is greedy and sex starved. 'But I only want sex with you'. 'Liar!' He splits her into different parts, pick pocketing the pride left in her to its last shred, but she stands there, erect and motionless, holding herself still like an inanimate object. The challenge of God is in her. Her feet are led. She recalls looking at something shiny on the pavement that she imagined must have fallen out of a ring or necklace of some pedestrian passing by. If someone had passed by she hadn't seen him, but she also knew Asad would never believe her. She holds on to her seat as the car almost flies off the road. He looks straight ahead and stretches his legs and arms out. He is roaring questions at her. She answers him in monosyllables, barely making a sound. Her body is shaking involuntarily and she looks ahead of her. He parks the car and drags her out with her hair. Today he will kill me, she thinks.

'You bitch, you fucking bitch. I should have known all along. You are always looking at men, aren't you? Answer me!'

'Yes, I do and that's because I am sure they have bigger ones than you do.'

She knows she will be punished but now wants to see her punishment. She will spit in its face. He drags her to the kitchen by her hair. He opens a drawer with one hand and takes out a meat knife.

'You see this, ha? I will cut your throat if you ever look at anyone else again.' She doesn't say anything. He keeps talking about his love for her and how much she has hurt him. Within minutes he is a different person. He starts crying and then begs for forgiveness.

'How could you do this to me, how could you? I love you so much. You are my life. Promise me you didn't do those things with other people.'

She tries to touch him, to make sure this is real but he pushes her away. 'Asad, I do love you, I swear I love you and I don't want to be with anyone else.'

'Promise Alya, do you promise you'll be with me forever and die with me.' He is sobbing.

'I promise.' She hugs his head.

'Oh Alya, you are my life.'

They have sex.

He gets up and opens his closet and takes out a bottle of vodka.

'Now my love, we will have the time of our lives. It's time I introduced you to blue dust.'

He pours out two glasses of vodka to the half mark and places them on his bedside table, which also has a lamp on it and a knife, to be used for various unknown purposes. He leaves for a couple of minutes. When he comes back Alya looks into his sad eyes and feels a rush of love towards him and she is ready for whatever he is to bring to her that night. She picks up one of the glasses and looks at the varicose liquid inside. He returns with a teaspoon and puts two blue tablets on the table and crushes them with the back of the spoon. He divides the powder into two portions and drops one portion in each glass. 'Drink this my love, your world will spin.'

Blue dust descends to its death in circular hostility to its world. It too has an inevitable fate.

He hands one of the glasses to her and she takes a sip.

Poison must taste like this, she thinks. She balks and Asad laughs. 'It happens in the beginning, don't worry, just keep drinking, slowly.'

She drinks it with purpose imagining it will kill her by the morning, but she says nothing obeying his instructions, telling herself that she has to trust him. The room spins on its axis. Cryptic scratches of a story mould themselves onto their empty bodies and she is fragmented. He asks if she feels good. She says she does. He switches the rest of the lights in the room off except for his red lamp. 'You don't have to worry Alya. I am going to be here to look after you, until we die.' She squeezes herself out of his arms and tells him she needs to lie down. He protrudes from every inch of his red room. She tries to talk about sex so that he stops telling her how much he loves her. It is a constant groan in her head. Definitions of things and needs fade by the time two hours have passed. She just wants to go to sleep to stop her head spinning. At some imprecise point in the evening she feels his fingers climb up between her legs and crawl into her vagina. The last thing she remembers is him telling her was how good she was at fucking him. 'The more it hurts, the more fun you'll have…' She wakes up the next morning in a pink bottle. The world is upside down.

ଓଃଌ

Devi held an informal weekly meeting where women would get together and talk about their various interpretations of scripture in the holy book. Usually one speaker gave a lecture and sometimes this would be followed by a discussion. On this particular day the speaker was a well-known religious figure and she had specified that she could only spare one hour for the lecture and then she would have to leave. Alya could hear the husky voice of a woman who sounded strong and frightening, an all-encompassing boom that made her sound larger than life. 'Today's discussion will be on sin.'

She climbed out of bed quickly before she missed something important. She tried to get up, but had to hold on to a chair in case she fell down again. The chemicals stung. She walked on a tight rope thinking of the grave look in both her parents' eyes if they had seen her like this. She felt sad, pathetic, unworthy of living. Her thoughts were interrupted by a powerful voice. The air resounded with her echo. Maybe that woman could help her, she was convinced this was a sign from God so she could seek forgiveness and assuage her own guilt, but the safest place Alya could think of right now was with Asad. Maybe he could explain it all to her; maybe she needed to cleanse herself in some way.

Those sitting in front of the woman, her disciples, were balls of cotton wool, rolled up in glass bulbs, each confined to her hell, while the woman on the dais carried on. Sing song sing song sing song. Good bad, good bad, good bad. All in her hands, in her control and the die rolled on and on in eternal somersaults... Her magnificence was iridescent and all consuming. The unquestionable authority in her voice told Alya there was truth in her conviction. She heard her telling her gathering (who were each firmly fixed to their own ground) the dangers of losing their purpose in life. 'What will happen to you in the hereafter? Isn't that far more important than this transitory existence we have here on earth. You must do what is right. You must not sin. You must listen to your husbands, remain modest in your ways and committed to your families. Your children and your husbands come first, but remember you too have rights. You must be taken good care of by your husbands. ...The words trailed on... Remember to cover yourselves, you are not for sale or for the eyes of other men...' She was erasing their lives gradually like numbers from a blackboard. By the end of her sermon, she had made their lives meaningless. Most of them had black hearts. What a God-like creature! Alya got closer; she wanted to see the woman who had more power than anyone she had ever met. She peeped from a chink in the door.

About twenty women sat randomly on the carpet, mostly cross-legged. Tea and biscuits were laid out in the adjoining dining room. An ant had almost reached the mouth of a woman but before she could eat it, it hid inside itself out of fear. The ant held up its hands in triumph and then rubbed them together fervently, whispering to another ant next to her. They knew. They had arrived at their ordained destination. The woman continued listening to her destiny. Most of her disciples including the ant woman wore a veil. The rest felt naked, ugly. Could God's messenger also hide her soul in her veil?

The great eagle (with salvation in her hands) sat perched on the dais. She had pink cheeks and a round face, tightly packing her in. The woman went on to list the different kinds of sin there were as if she had heard Alya's thoughts. Alya counted her own sins as at least nine out of ten. She was now telling her defenseless listeners, how torturous hell fire was and how their bodies would roast slowly over the hottest fire imaginable. 'It is 100 times hotter than the fire we know of in this world.' Softly softly, my love, *the gentle pitter-patter of rain leaves a smudge where I left you and there is no place left to go now, my sweet God. He is with me in the silence between your words.* 'If you do not follow the path of God, you will burn in hell for a thousand years. The choice is yours!' Her voice was calm. One stroke, this way and that. One stroke back and one stroke forward. Calm. The rebirth of roses imminent.

Their choices had gone. Alya could now see the woman's pitying eyes fixed sternly on the terrified lot in front of her. She looked at them as if she had just fed them their last meal, henceforth they would begin their walk to the after life, cleansed and fat with new knowledge and devotion. They were unmovable, in the middle of a bleeding silence that spread rapidly through a crowd she was so intimate with today but didn't even know the day before. She started to walk away, her huge, majestic veil sweeping the floor behind. The living dead dispersed slowly. They hardly had the strength to leave the room. Horror. Horror. And one final gasp. The ants also went home.

Alya's vomit was near the surface, she could smell it. She had to hide it from the rest, so she ran into the bathroom just in time for it to slip past the others and buried herself in the flush for the next half an hour. She was deeply engaged in the mental act of self-mutilation, pushing her fingers deep into her throat in case any scraps of food had remained in her gullet, when Devi called out to her. The smell of her vomit kept her alert, so she didn't flush for a while and stared at the ripples in the brown watery abyss beneath her. She hated Devi for everything she had put her mother through. She wanted to cut open her indolent face and slice it into pieces with her regained strength after the vomit had come out. She didn't answer her and stayed inside until she heard her walking away. It was all her fault. Why didn't she know what was happening to her or anyone else around her. Or did she know and was she simply ignoring it to keep things steady– just to make her life easier. Sonia had started staying out as much as she could because she was tired of seeing her sister with Asad all the time. 'What is it with you two?' she had asked her, 'don't you ever get enough of each other.' Alya had no idea how much Sonia knew and Sonia didn't let on either.

After rising from the comfort of the washroom Alya rushed to Asad for refuge. She knocked on the door lightly. There was no answer. 'Asad?' fear singed her. She could smell vodka. 'Asad!' Something was wrong. The doorknob turned and his hand grabbed her and pulled her in. The door slammed shut. Glass, like chopped water covered the floor. Broken bits of red glass hid between the floorboards. Only the frame of the mirror she looked into the previous night was intact. It made her sad. Torn clothes and sheets littered the carpet. Blood bursts in my head. She looked at Asad's face. His eyes were red, swollen. He hugged her, suddenly. 'Alya, promise you'll never say that again?' That woman was right. This was all her fault, she had almost killed him. She couldn't remember what she had said the previous night and she dreaded the answer too much to ask. She apologized without knowing why. 'I am sorry Asad.' Her small heart beat frantically.

The next morning he was a new man cracking jokes and showing her his boxing techniques. It was almost like when she was a child again. She had her Asad bhai back again. But when night came, Asad bhai was gone.

Asad and Alya were in a constant drugged haze of violence and betrayal covering decades in hours; the days fused together to paint scenes of a marriage doomed to failure; other nights they promised each other an undying love worth dying for. A day seemed like a lifetime, yet sometimes hours passed in seconds. He accused her of infidelity repeatedly and she begged him for forgiveness. After some time they started having sex less frequently and she fought with him for not wanting to be with her anymore. He said he couldn't help it; he wouldn't get an erection that often anymore. Valium, vodka and 'love' were crusting their veins. She became a fanatic about those days and nights with him. At fourteen she was forty.

As an adult those nights came back to her over and over again. She kept an empty Valium bottle with Asad's dried-up blood in it for years to come because it was witness to the fact that he still loved her wherever he was and that his love was eternal and not unreal like she sometimes thought it was. He had given it to her as a souvenir of his love.

They are water babies, dipped in the golden sun under a turquoise sky on a big round day. Alya is awkward and uncomfortable with her body, so she laughs all the time, making a joke out of everything he says. She wants to run away with him, start a new life. He is teasing her, playing with her hair. The branches on the mango trees are heavy with mangoes. The green rustle of diamond leaves grows louder amplifying her feelings of excitement. He is resting his head on her lap. She tries not to get aroused but she can't help it. Asad come back home… please my love.

She became addicted to Valium for years after leaving Asad, and couldn't get out of bed without having four or five tablets in the morning. The drug created a haze she became comfortable in. She had thought she and Asad could live on and on like that forever, she couldn't ever have imagined it would ever end. She took a stock of Valium back to Zakar with her, hidden in her shoes and bags. When she missed him too much she took Valium. When she didn't, she took even more to remember what it was like when they were together. Then one day Zaib found the tablets. Zaib looked pale that day, but didn't really say too much. She didn't talk to Alya for a few days. It was strange how she didn't question Alya about where she had got them from either. She simply took her aside and said, 'Alya please don't ever touch those tablets again. I won't have that in this house.' Ammi was odd. As she grew older, she knew ammi less and less and began to feel she was losing her to something more sinister, something bigger than them all.

She missed Asad less as time wore on; initially she looked forward to the planned visit the year following the 'golden' summer, but Zaib refused to go, saying she wanted to spend the summer just with her daughters and Hassan. Alya hated her for it at the time, but a year later she was grateful. She couldn't even remember Asad's features clearly anymore and she tried desperately to recall what his nose or mouth, looked like. She also had no memory left of certain events that summer with him though he remained an icon, the mentor she couldn't abandon because he was an intrinsic part of her.

Despite the repercussions of those events on the rest of her life, she often justified Asad's actions in her own mind. There were no myths to be told or heard. Everything was real, juxtaposed with the self-denying will that says what happens is all fantasy; she knew it was true and permanent. What she had left of Asad was the *idea* of a spotless life, the blanket nights she and Asad surrounded themselves with, the perfect marriage and three children they'd named in conversations on *happier* days when they laughed for hours. The majestic garden of their great and wise grandfather stayed, but Asad was swept back into the dark abyss of the unknown. She could no longer think of him as a person who actually ever existed and for the next few years every time she saw him she pretended in her mind that she hardly knew him. Strangely, it worked. One night, she burnt his letters and told Sonia she never wanted to see him again. Sonia ate three bowls of ice cream that night and took her sister to see a movie. She told her she was proud of her and hugged her over and over again.

'Thank God we are rid of that bastard, that abuser, that thing that should be in jail!' She could have killed him over and over again, but Alya had always stopped her from saying anything, 'think of what would happen to ammi, to Devi khala, to everyone. Please let it be. I will be all right I promise.'

Asad had a failed marriage and an ex-wife and two children who had abandoned him, did she feel she had some sort of peace? Today, as she stands by her mother who is dreaming of some distant land, lost with her fairies and elves, was she really able to wipe it away? Asad was gone but the unique smell of vodka and blue dust stretched through her days, her blue-powder days of measuring the margins of death moment by moment and savouring the tragedy of life while she still had time. She had managed to sift out the necessary parts to live and today she was a stronger person.

Alya married fifteen years after her first night with Asad. She began something new that lasted long after Zaib and Devi and long after the unjust acts of love caused by the proprietor of souls. Was Asad right about his strange philosophies? Some days when she thought about that time in her life she felt she had gained the invaluable simplicity of an experience, no matter how painful or *wrong* that was. Other mornings she cried after having sex with her husband and there was no end to the memory of Asad's hands on her; she lived with his words still teaching her right from wrong, good from bad. She told herself he was a criminal as Sonia had said he was and that what he had done could not be forgiven, then why did she still miss him sometimes, how could she still believe in his ideals? She questioned her own sense of morality. She was sad for her parents, thinking of ammi that day she arrived back from her holiday not knowing that her daughter had changed forever. All she had wanted to do was to hold ammi and cry but she couldn't, ammi could never know, it would be too much, too much for her to bear. Ammi had to remain unharmed, untouched by her sin.

Alya stroked her mother's jet-black hair. She looked like a child, sleeping so peacefully in her bed. Can't we stay together like this forever? She had to help her, make her see that no matter what happens in life, life itself is a gift and has to be lived. Life is beautiful, just like ammi said it was. Should I call Devi khala? She had a right to know, even though Alya felt she was partly responsible for her mother's condition. She had to do it. She picked up the phone, after three rings someone picked up. It was him. She wanted to scream at him, tell him how much she hated him, how much pain he had caused the family, but instead she just said, 'Khaloo it's me, Alya.'

'Oh Alya beta, how are you?'

She was short. 'I am fine. Can I speak to Devi khala?'

'Yes of course.' Charming as always when it came to others.

Devi sounded happier. Of course she would be, *he* was home after months and even after everything he had done she still loved him – the dutiful subservient wife that she was. It had cost her, it had cost her mother. Bitch.

'Devi khala, ammi is here with me. She doesn't seem to be too well. Can you come over?'

'Oh no, is it the same thing again?'

'Look khala I really don't know, can you just come over?'

'Yes of course, I will be there within fifteen minutes.' Devi lived only fifteen minutes away but it was a deliberate choice on Alya's part to meet her only once in several months. Her resentment towards Devi began a long time ago. It had begun when Zaib had told her the truth about Devi's situation. Zaib had just got off the phone to Devi. She looked shaken. Alya was standing in front of her.

'Ammi what is the matter?'

'Nothing.'

'Ammi please tell me, I am old enough to know.'

'It's Devi khala, she is sick.'

'What is wrong with her, she is always sick. Please don't tell me you have to go and visit her again.'

'You don't understand, it's that snake husband of hers, he won't stop until she dies.'

ఆ

Devi was pregnant with her first son.

'This baby will make the difference. They say when a woman has a baby the husband automatically comes back to his wife.'

Zaib wanted to take her into her arms and keep her there forever, her innocent Devi.

'Devi, we know that's not fair and you know it won't happen. You have to be realistic. You are young; you can abort this baby and divorce him.'

'Divorce? And live a life of disgrace like our parents? Never. The baby will bring us together. He is just lost at the moment. You know how army men are, old habits don't just go. I am his wife after all.'

When the baby was born he spent one week at home and then left again. Devi saw less and less of him. She spent her life trying to figure out what evil she had done and was being punished for. Asad's brother was born next and Devi kept herself busy with the children. When her father became ill, she was in Abbottabad where her husband had been transferred and which was several miles from Lahore. It made it difficult for her to visit daddy so she couldn't come home for months after he was diagnosed with cancer. By the time she got back he was bed ridden. The premonition of death lingered on the doors of the house. She recalled walking in to the house and hearing Zaib's giggles sliding up the sides of the walls. The corners whispered ghosts littering the streets of her memory with the familiar path of her chequered youth. She saw herself run into a room and disappear into the walls, she looked eight or nine and unlike herself. Devi told me thirty years later that it was the most desolate house she had ever seen, with just a nuance of its former days, its grandeur lost in some casual talk on the outside about the family inside fading fast. There was no sound except the faint footsteps of children, unwilling to yield to the end of time. She called out to the cook, who was the one solitary figure in that creaking mansion she once called home; *he* was always present, always affirming the existence of a home that he was an intrinsic part of, protecting its sanctity from foreigners and those wanting to harm the integrity of the family within.

Baba Badar stood at the same juncture, firm in his commitment and the belief that he still had a home. His faith was worth admiring, Devi thought, observing his unchanged rustic features and welcoming gestures that came so naturally to him. Devi felt as if she had nothing natural left in her, her life had so little meaning that she was always pretending now. She looked at him again, carefully. He hadn't aged either. He was still warm, emerging from his smoky, clanging kitchen, brimming with the aroma of curry, fruit *chaats* and rich sauces, new recipes in the making. Baba Badar was the skeleton body holding up the house without touching it, without trying. That was *his* magic and he remained unflinching in his faith to *his* family. He had found a way to keep the house alive despite death hovering on every shelf. He was lucky.

Devi found what she was looking for as soon as she saw him. He had a dishcloth on his shoulder and he was wearing the same faded apron mummy had given him fifteen years ago. The familiar odour of garlic and curry tracked him down in the palace of ghosts and Devi knew when she saw him that that this was where she truly belonged, with Baba Badar by her side, in her old mansion even if it was in ruins. She wanted to hold him and smell him forever; she wanted him to be a part of her and look after her for the rest of her life so that he could protect her too in *his* arms, so she could remain unharmed and pure like the walls of his making. The man was the embodiment of the spirit of *her* house, the house where the rooms trembled with the laughter of two children buried somewhere in its walls, the house she would revisit again and again even after the death of those who lived there. That's when it occurred to her that she wasn't really there to see her father or to see Baba Badar or for that matter her mother, she was there to see history face to face, to remind her that her life was not without reason, that people are borne out of something important, something that has a place in the world.

'Devi beti, my child, how are you? Where have you been, it's so long now! You just disappeared. You even forgot your old baba.' He almost ran to meet her.

Devi bent down for him to kiss her forehead. Baba Badar had come as a young boy to be trained as a cook for a few months. His parents were going to take him to Karachi after his training to find work in the hustle and bustle of the most commercial city in Pakistan. At that time people went to the capital to find their fortunes. Somehow Baba Badar never left their home. His parents had gone more than thirty years ago and Baba Badar had stayed behind. He was such an intrinsic part of their family now that no one even asked how he ended up staying.

Devi walked into her father's room. She saw him lying there alone forgotten by the world. She blamed Zaib for leaving him on his own like that. Where was she now when he needed her the most? She was angry.

She whispered, 'Daddy.'

'Devi, is it you?'

'Yes daddy, I arrived just now.'

'Please forgive me Devi. I wish we had given you a better life.'

'Oh it is not your fault. For God's sake don't speak like that.'

'The rest of them are out there conquering the world. You can still do it Devi, it's not too late.' There was a little twinkle in his eye when he said it and Devi smiled.

After dinner Devi and Zaib were in the bedroom.

'Why have you left him alone?'

'I haven't.'

'This is when he needs you most.'

'I can't Devi, I will kill him even faster if I stay with him; my love will kill him. Don't you understand he needs to die in peace.'

'You can, you have to.'

'Where are you these days?'

'Still struggling. I can't do it.'

'It's not good enough.'

'That's because you don't know what it's like.'

'Why don't you leave him?'

'Oh everything is so simple for you, isn't it Zaib?'

'Why don't you talk to mummy?'

'About what, she is busy playing cards.'

'She is busy trying to be sane in this house!'

'What have we done?'

'Nothing, it's just that he needs you.'

Zaib shut herself off and left the room.

When Devi saw him dead she couldn't help but think, *maybe you deserved this, maybe you got what you had to*. And then she cried until there were no more tears left.

ఌ

13

Babies

Zaib let's have a baby.' Hassan had been hinting he wanted a baby for almost a year now, and Zaib had deliberately been avoiding the topic. When he said it this time, he said it with finality and she knew it had to be done. Hassan had always loved children; and she wanted what he loved even though motherhood was not what she had ever wanted, even the thought of it paralyzed her. She did not harbour any great affection for children in general. The horror started all over again. *The horror of a caterpillar turning into a butterfly inside her.* For days she had nightmares where she saw dogs ripping her legs away and pools of blood on sidewalks surreptitiously waiting for her to step by. The next few months were agonizing, just the thought of conceiving terrified her. She thought of the baby as a worm burrowing into her body building its unwelcome home inside *her* womb. The thought of an intruder in their lives terrified her.

It took a year for Zaib to become pregnant. When she saw her urine result she kept staring at the two stripes on the strip of white paper for a long time and then she started crying. In the beginning she cried herself to sleep. She called the fetus, *the octopus child* in her mind. It was an unwanted creature, a bacteria feeding on her insides. As it grew it took away more and more from her. For the first three months she felt sick all the time so she couldn't eat and her head ached constantly. She was also urinating every few hours and at least three times a night which made her feel like a decrepit unable to control her own bodily functions. The doctor recommended she have more fruit and milk, both of which she despised.

Zaib resented the creature inside her that dictated her life. She wasn't Zaib any more, she was the thing and Zaib as 'one', the beast sharing *her* vessel with her. Although they told her, her pregnancy was no more difficult than most women's, she complained incessantly and told Hassan several times how much she felt like tearing it out of her body and throwing it away.

'Zaib, you can't feel that way about your own baby?'

'I want it to go to hell. It's caused me nothing but misery!'

Hassan felt defensive about the growing fetus inside her and developed an alliance with his unborn baby, which lasted well beyond her birth.

In her fifth month, Zaib felt the baby kick for the first time. It was the first time she felt a little protective about the baby and gradually as the kicks became more frequent, her protectiveness turned into joy. By her eighth month she started secretly waiting for the kicks and if she didn't feel one for she would secretly worry.

Alya was a cranky baby. When she was a little older she knew she had been a handful. But then she had good reason to be. She often felt excluded by her mother, ammi was too self consumed, too busy being cradled by her father, or trying to get his attention, or trying to please him – little as she was it all seemed to be about him. There was a clear divide. Ammi and abba on one side and she on the other.

Then one day after an immense amount of pain the voice of an Arab nurse told Zaib it was finally over and she had had another baby girl, 'You have a beeuthifool baby gurrl.' Alya ran to her mother. She was four at the time. 'Ammi, this is our baby, *henna*?'

'Yes my darling, she is all ours.'

They named her Sonia. For Alya she was absolutely perfect. This one is all mine she thought. From the moment she saw her she adored her, her little flawless angel with soft pink cheeks and perfect hands and feet.

Zaib watched her stomach become flatter over the next few months and thanked God she didn't get the dreaded stretch marks (one of her mother's sisters frequently displayed her stretch marks as a proud sign of motherhood, she had mothered six children, all of whom Zaib had despised). The baby cried all night and kept both parents awake while either one or the other tried to rock her to sleep. With time they settled down but as the girls got older, Zaib found it increasingly difficult to share Hassan with them. She'd often say to him, 'Do you love me as much as you love them?'

He would sound annoyed. 'Zaib, they are our children. I love them as our children,' and then he would soften, 'Zaib my angel, I adore you; you know that and no one can take your place.' He held her in his arms and put his hand on her head almost like a father cajoling his daughter.

One step back. The world shrink down down more and more. Daddy and me on a pink pink daisy.

Alya had picked up on her mother's jealousy and became even more remorseless in showering her father with affection. But when Sonia was born and as she grew older Alya also noticed that they had a compatibility that she could not compete with. Initially she tried to but as she matured she too became closer to her mother. She tapped into her mother's silent suffering, and her instinct was to protect her first. Zaib also depended on Alya sensing her daughter's silent understanding, her quiet support. She clung to her as if she were her only saviour in a world where she was losing everything else. At times Alya wanted to protect her, yet she angered her so much with her constant craving for love. She wanted to stand in the way of anything that tried to hurt her because she knew what she could not express to the world, she felt her pain and her growing uneasiness, yet she wanted her to somehow break out of it and reclaim her world.

As time passed Zaib and Hassan began to argue more often about trivialities. The same things tended to come up again and again. They were mainly Hassan spending too much time at work and Devi's frequent breakdowns. The children inevitably took sides. Usually Sonia argued in her father's defense, 'He has to work. I mean what does she want to do, sit in his lap all day and ask him to tell her how much daddy loves her?!' Alya knew Ammi was losing the battle.

Hassan resented Devi's influence on Zaib. Every time Devi had a breakdown Zaib rushed to her rescue and when she returned Hassan would have to put her together again. On one of her visits to Devi, Zaib called him from Pakistan.

'Hassan I must stay here for a few months. That bastard has left her and says he won't be back until the summer. She is talking like a child, how can I leave her like this?'

'Well that's just not our problem. What about your children, our children? What are they supposed to do? We have a family too Zaib.'

Zaib had come back reluctantly and when she did she was morose and thoughtful. Her nightmares became worse....

Sonia had jumped into the well to find her doll. Zara was Sonia's bedroom doll, a porcelain doll with cold eyes and peach smiling lips. Her hair was steel grey, and her heart was ice, you could see it beat like the unshakable fear of impending doom causing the familiar ambience of caterpillar horror around Zaib. Zaib could not bear to be in the same room as her for long. There was a cold breeze between her legs and matchstickmen came back again.

'Sonia grab the rope!' Sonia had just realized she was in danger.

'Mummy I can't see you,' Zaib became paralysed with fear, oh God what will I do, God can't do this, God can do anything. Hassan arrived in time and Sonia was pulled away from heaven's gate. (Probably heaven, thought Zaib, because she was a child and children cannot sin.) But Zara could not be saved and somewhere in her head she always felt she had a dead friend with her. Zara had left her too early.

Zaib woke up lost, 'Where is Sonia? Is she alright?'

'Zaib, please I beg you not to go back to Lahore again. Devi is ruining our lives ... that neurotic woman! Sonia is fine, but your nightmares get so much worse when you come back from seeing her. This has to stop.'

'Hassan please, don't ask me for what I am incapable of. You know how much I love her. I can't just leave her to her destiny. You know she needs help.'

But Zaib did listen to him and for a year she stayed home away from Devi, trying to let her solve her own problems. Zaib's life was swept up by her sister, her children, her worries for them and the mundane duties that had to be performed day to day, but at the same time she missed the days when it was just the two of them. Even now her eyes would fill up with tears when she thought of Hassan and her in the old days.

Sonia found her mother's sporadic bursts of resentment towards them hard to forgive. As she grew older Alya tried to understand

Zaib's insecurities and began to feel her father drifting away from the family. Though she was very close to him as a child in recent years he had become someone she looked up to from a distance. Ammi was her priority because she thought ammi could survive less.

'I saw the wonder in her words, a sort of heaven in the things she said and did,' she told Sonia when they were women. 'Our father married a woman who didn't change, she was always the same sixteen year old he had brought home to his parents, then why did he expect her to become different? It is unfair.' She had watched her mother sleeping soundly one morning. The previous night had been difficult and after Zaib and Hassan had fought for hours, Hassan had finally packed a bag and walked out. He came back in the morning looking strained and gloomy.

That summer day when ignorant flies buzzed past the window of Zaib's room while she slept in her bed, Sonia knew it was just a matter of time.

One night, unexpectedly, Zara came back to Zaib.

She dreamt of an old haveli. There is a sweet shuffle, the sitar is playing to the wind, the raj of the Mughals is at its peak, breezy music sweeps the lawns, hinged on an ancestral memory, crackling sounds echo, like a scratched LP with two hundred years of dust to prove its wisdom and worth. Dancing girls dance like birds waiting to be fed, their flat empty bellies moving back and forth to the rhythms of their nawabs' desires. She can smell their soft, clean dupattas, fluttering in the purple wind carrying them to the edge of reason. She longs to touch them even when she knows they are buried somewhere where she can't reach them. The sound of their payal jingling in my head, cutting through time. Zaib peeps through the door of the nawab's wife's room. She is a queen dressed for her king, waiting for him on her bed, he will make love to her and go to his own room until the next time, but she doesn't care. The cream silk pillow covers are laced with maroon tassels and she is playing with them with her fingers, her legs sprawled over the pillows. She is stroking herself preparing for her nawab. And Zaib knows she is Zara, beautiful and cold. She will make love to her king that night with the cruelty of a woman who doesn't love her man, and yet he would never find out he's been cheated. He in turn, would come to her bed with the same love for her he gives all his beautiful women. But as he comes close to her, the dream changes abruptly, the corroded crust of the haveli lies bare and charred cattle bones cover its grounds, Zaib is standing in its hallway of dead sounds. She can barely see it through the brown mist, and a scene from an old Charlie Chaplin movie flashes through her mind (she thinks she saw it with daddy once). She knows the haveli has a hundred rooms and sees half-open wooden cupboards and doors as if the last generation that lived in the haveli had died in the middle of something happening, something in motion. She can feel that something important had not been done yet, something had been left before its time. She walks through some of the cobwebbed rooms one by one and all she sees are rows and rows of beige coloured cloth dolls. Some of them are face to face, conspiring, some are holding hands, while others stare starkly ahead as a warning. Unlike Zara they are not erect like a ballerina. Their eyes are coloured beads like the sea. They are waiting for something: shocked into stillness. Hundreds of women suddenly appear, they are sitting on the floor, among the dolls, and in the veranda and the rooms, spilling over into the present, exchanging faces with people Zaib knows, for moments here and there, old and bent, brooding eyes talking plans. Their voices muffle and merge into each other. I circled the body (in awe of death) of the first husband who was killed, in this haveli the women had always won. They are talking about the dolls, they are discussing which kind of spirit to put in which doll. Suddenly Zaib realizes the dolls are about to come to life and thousands of dolls would emerge from the rooms. They are about to start moving. TERROR makes her head spin.

Zaib is outside looking up at the divided sky. She looks up. Zara, the doll is alive and she is sitting on the moon while it begins to crack. The haveli is in ruins. The world is silver and daddy picks her up. Are you all right my love?

❧

A year later Zaib was back from Pakistan after another one of Devi's *episodes*. She was still hazy when she arrived at the airport in Zakar. Hassan had been waiting at the airport for two hours because the flight was delayed. He looked tired and fed up. He handed her a bouquet of roses and smiled, but she could see it wasn't a smile from the heart and the roses suddenly lost their charm. She had forgotten the desert heat in less than a month and the humidity stung her face as soon as she stepped outside. But then she heard the *azaan*... just before she saw Hassan and she felt that everything might just be all right.

In the car the conversation was stilted.

'So did you miss me daddy?'

He remained quiet for a couple of seconds as if thinking of an answer. Zaib became increasingly agitated.

'Well?'

'Do you think we should go on holiday, we haven't been yet, have we?'

What was wrong? Was he bored with her?

'You look distracted.'

'I've been very busy at work that's all.'

'Daddy you did miss me?'

'Of course I missed you Zaib.'

He *was* bored she was sure of that and so she was careful with every word she spoke, 'Shall we go out for dinner tonight?'

Waiting for an answer her eyes remained fixed on the dashboard while she thought of what to say next. Hassan looked straight ahead. But he couldn't bear her helplessness for long. He broke the silence, 'How was Devika?'

'Daddy I think she is becoming a fanatic. What will I do if that happens?'

'Zaib you have to let her be, it's not in your hands and it's not your fault, she has to be what she wants.'

She looked out at the desert, now arid and lifeless and felt hopeless, her Devi was so changed and she could do nothing. She glanced at Hassan for help; he knew she would, but this time he didn't offer her anything; there was no other way to help her.

'Dad we will go to dinner tonight, won't we?'

'Yes Zaib we will, we will go to dinner.'

But Zaib knew him better than a church knows its cherub. Ultimately she softened at his innocence. At least he was trying. She knew he wanted to help her, but then things change like one rainfall from the next and the change is sadly, inevitable. He could hardly help it, like Devi couldn't help living the life she was or like her father couldn't help dying when the cancer had eaten him. But she carried on wishing, dreaming, chasing hope.

ꟹ

14

Brian

Alya remembered Brian, vaguely. He had kind blue eyes. When he smiled it sent ripples around his mouth, which made him look much older than his years. She wished she could see Brian's reassuring smile just one more time. That might help her and her mother. Zaib had first noticed Brian because of his hands. They seemed to hold a record like the eternal moon held a record of the world. They were inoffensive and impeccable, innocent and concerned. Above all they emanated a kind of peace.

The few months before she met Brian, she had been particularly lonely. The girls were busy at school and Hassan was busy at work. She started visiting the British Council Library where fiction was limited but she managed to find a few interesting books she'd not read before. A couple of months had passed and the library had begun to look dreary with its tube light shadows and dusty shelves, when she noticed the man who gave out the books at the counter.

She hoped he might have noticed her too. It was a Monday and daddy was going to be late. The library was about to close. She struck up a conversation with him. He was renewing her book, *A Pair of Blue Eyes.*

'I like Hardy very much. Have you read *Jude*?'

'No but I'd like to. We need better stuff in here, I've just started working here but I'll see what I can do.'

They got to know each other better over the next few weeks. He told her of his travels all over the world. He had been to the Far East,

America New Zealand, Africa. She listened with wonder. 'Didn't you get attached to any of these places?'

'Yes in a way, but I love travelling.'

He didn't seem unsettled and spoke fondly about the people he had met on his travels and yet he seemed distant from his environment in a strange way. This had just become a way of life for him, Zaib thought. In spite of that he seemed vulnerable like a child in new surroundings and yet there was a strange contradiction in him, he looked troubled somewhere inside. He had sad eyes. She couldn't figure it out. He intrigued her in so many ways. She told him about life in Pakistan, a place he said he would love to visit. He invited her for tea.

'Daddy can I go and see Brian for tea this afternoon?'

She had mentioned him to Hassan before, actually several times.

'Zaib you don't need to take permission from me.'

He looked pensive.

She had locked into something.

I can hear dad and mama screaming in the next room and that is what causes this lump in my throat. I can't move my feet…. they are too heavy… almost detached from the rest of my body. I can see my father's eyes murdering my mother over and over again. The doorbell rings.

'Zaib!' she shrieks, 'answer that!'

My feet are released by the sound of my mother's voice and they run to the door. It's difficult to speak: 'It's Reha-nna Khala.'

Rehana Khala finds her own way to the lounge. She takes off her shoes and puts her feet up on the sofa. 'Beta go and get me some water, will you, it's so hot outside and why are you wearing that horrible frock, you are becoming a big girl now you know, your legs should not be bare.'

'I like my dress.'

'Oh stop being so insolent and listen to your elders. Now go and get me a glass of water.'

I walk to the kitchen and tell the cook to get her a glass of water. I hear mother walking out of her room. The door closes behind her. I see my father dying on his bed. Mummy is taking quick steps towards the lounge. I think mummy and Rehana Khala are conspiring against dad and me. Mother suddenly becomes cheerful at the sight of her sister and I can hear them laughing and talking. I want to go and see father but my feet are stuck again and I am also scared of what I might see.

'Zaib, Zaib come here immediately!' It is the voice of my mother. I am summoned to the ballroom. Rehana Khala has a seductive look in her eye and a secret smile lingers round her lips.

'Zaib, were you rude to your khala?' Her gaze is fixed on my lips.

'Zaib, answer me.' A grey swan and blinding sunshine rush through my mind.

'I just said I like my dress.'

'You are not supposed to argue with your elders, do you understand?! Now apologize.'

'No I won't.'

'Zaib you are asking for it.'

The snake joins in, 'Just like her father.'

'Zaib I am speaking to you.'

'Her father is the same, willful and stupid, typical Muslim.'

'Do not talk about my father like that.'

'How dare you!' almost in unison.

I can feel my hair being torn out at the roots and flashes of Rehana Khala with a satisfied grin on her face. After it is over, I run to my father's room. He pulls me in and quickly shuts the door. 'Oh Zaib, why do you even speak to them?'

'I can't keep quiet dad, Rehana khala was saying things about you.'

'It doesn't matter Zaib. We both know it's not true, so why should we care. As for your mother she loves you very much, she is just angry right now.'

I can't cry but instead sit with my father for a while thinking about what dad might do to mama one day and about the things I want dad to do to mama sometimes. I am woken up by my mother who is sitting on my bed.

'Zaib, are you all right?'

'I don't want to talk to you.'

'Zaib I love you, you are my child but you must learn to respect your elders.'

'I will not let anyone talk about my father like that.'

'It's always your father, your father, what about me and my feelings? My feelings.'

'Why don't you stop them?'

'Now wash your face and come to dinner in a civilized fashion.'

The mirror closes its doors.

Is my father still alive? Yes my dad, the one who has lived a long time now in the grass between the blades of grass smiling in the winter and between the hours where closets hide old specks of dust far from the resounding chatter of crickets outside. It disturbs me this cone that is so full of coldness and sugar tells me my teeth will rot with microscopic organisms I will never see burrowing their under-nourished protrusions into my white teeth. Now when the summer is rife with flies screening the tips of my fingers with their greedy heads moving mechanically from side to side I realize that my teeth will save my soul in the ground of its choosing and that the cone and I have nothing to worry about... ... ...

Suddenly her head became untangled again.

'Daddy, did you say I could have tea with Brian?'

'Yes of course you can.'

The day he came to visit her was the first of many visits. Brian bought her white tube-roses. The pungent smell of the flowers filled the house. She could see his hands in every room. She began thinking of him in bed in the mornings just after waking up. He was a gypsy, a man without a plan and that fascinated her, how free and wild he was, how truly enlightened! He had no master plan. 'Is it ever like we plan anything anyway,' he had told her. Brian told her anecdotes about his travels and she listened intently captivated by his stories. In Africa he worked for WHO, in India he taught English to adults in a small town near Delhi. He had also been to Rome and Paris where famous painters and artists had made love and seen miracles. He had visited Venice during the carnival and he told her about the spectacular gowns and theatrical masks people wore, lovers drinking champagne and dancing on the streets, abandoned by thoughts of the future or past. Brian represented another world, a new world of pictures unfolded in front of her. She was in awe of the sincerity of the Greek islands and the proud erections of the pyramids, eternal and unshakable in their conviction to preserve a piece of history: and it was Brian who held a part of that history in his hands. She was proud of his life! But she was scared too. Was he fickle? Any man who didn't stay in one place for long must be. Did he not suffer for places and people?

He seemed so accepting, bearing life's troubles with a carefree lightness she found frightening. But as she watched him over the next few weeks, she noticed something new and it was then that she was convinced he cared; it was the way he spoke, there was this dip in his tone at the end of some of his sentences and those faint wrinkles around the corner of his mouth that she had noticed when she first saw him which told her he suffered just like her, just like others, and that she was therefore, safe. *She was safe.* She imagined in another life he would have been a monk, loving and patient, carrying the burden of life with a smile.

She had hardly known him a month and she had no idea what he did for a living in all those organizations he worked for, yet he seemed such an intrinsic part of her already.

Hassan came home late one night. Zaib was lying in bed staring at the ceiling. She was focusing on a crack in the ceiling wondering whether it was real.

'Hassan why are you always so late?'

She hadn't called him Hassan for a while now.

'What's on your mind?' he asked taking off his socks.

'I was just thinking of Brian's hands. They are so wrinkly and artistic at the same time. They are speaking hands.'

She heard Hassan get up.

'Smelly feet! Can I smell your toes dad?'

He was quiet.

'Dad, can't I smell your feet? You know I love the sweaty smell between your toes.'

'Let's sleep, it's late.'

He felt cheated, but said nothing. For a long time after she had gone to sleep he watched her, perplexed, anxious.

Two days later Zaib was getting dressed for dinner at the German Ambassador's house. She looked resplendent in her red sari and ruby necklace.

'Daddy I am nervous. I don't know anyone there.'

'I hardly know anyone either. Just make polite conversation, we'll be back soon. I just have to show my face there.'

'I'll do my best.' Her legs were trembling out of nervousness.

At the party there was a butterfly the colour of the ocean on a daisy, pink one minute and as the matchstick people swept the floor, blue the next. It came and sat on her shoulder for just a second and that reminded her of a great big river where fish swim restlessly. Ape-men laughed their days at night. They retreated under the carpet when the ambassador and his huge Adam's apple walked up to her.

'So young lady, I hope you are having a good time.'

She was shaken out of her stupor and at a loss for words for a few seconds, and then, 'I am fine, thanks.'

He smiled knowingly and made a welcoming gesture to the next guest. Zaib was relieved that he had left her and began her escape across the room to Hassan. On the way she saw Sophie, the ambassador's wife making her way to the bar, whispering something in his ear. She turned around and looked at her. Were they talking about her? Zaib clenched her fists with a syringe fear.

Next, the collision of a seagull in flight with a brigade of voices stunned her. She saw a black widow in the eyes of a woman climb out and up the blue dress of another.

The mutual enmity between people pushed her to the brink of insanity. She needed an escape. Mummy's crystal room and the blue smoke ...

'Hassan, can I have a drink?' She had never touched alcohol.

'Of course but just be careful, don't have too much.'

She asked for a glass of wine and took a sip. She winced and coughed. The second sip was easier. Zaib drank almost a bottle of wine that night holding daddy's hand most of the time and telling him how much she loved him. The next morning her head was a ball of lead and she wished she'd never touched the stuff.

At night she had a nightmare again ...

She falls on her back and hits the trampoline. The children start to laugh.

'Princess Zaib is not hurt, is she?'

Her arms and legs go stiff and she can't move. 'Mummy I can't move.'

She is shaking on the trampoline. Look look, she is so funny!

The teacher turns around to join in, a collaborator in the attempt to murder her again, 'Zaib you look silly, get up this instant!' Silly is in her blood.

'Zaib open your eyes, Zaib!'

'Zaib snap out of this, Zaib!'

Mama where are you? Mama? Can I be born again so I can be big once more. Saira grabs her neck. The ashtray stained with grey-black ash escapes the old cigar of daddy's mouth, a gaping urn echoing in his big empty room. Zaib it's daddy, you are home now.

ঙ্গ

Hassan came home from work with a big black ant on his shoe. The ant held on as long as it could but eventually was forced to let go. He looked pensive. Two days ago he had received a message that his mother had had a stroke.

'Are you going to go then? But what will I do? The children have school.'

'So, so what Zaib? So bloody what? She is my mother, I have to go!'

His words brought her guilt to the surface and silenced her for hours. She saw him go through the motions of taking his shoes off, changing his clothes, washing his face, hoping that in between all that he might notice her, but he didn't. That evening he slept with his back towards her.

'Daddy?'

His silence reminded her of her days in the convent: the convent at night.

'Daddy, are you still angry?'

'Ammi died this morning.'

She brushed her hand across his face and cradled his head in her arms, kissing his forehead in bed, taking care of the little things he needed. At last she felt needed.

15

Home

Hassan and Zaib had just returned to Pakistan after a two-month holiday in America.

Hassan looked anxious.

'What's wrong daddy?'

'I want to leave Zakar.'

'What do you mean?'

'The girls are young women now, that society is not healthy for them besides they should know something about their own culture too before it's too late.'

'There are boys here in Pakistan as well, Hassan. You can't protect them forever.'

'Zaib, you haven't noticed anything strange about Alya, have you?' He said it quietly as if deep down he didn't really want her to hear but he had to say it anyway.

She looked at him and said glibly, 'No.'

Hassan was relieved.

'I just think the girls are too old now and they should learn more about their own culture. We've made our money Zaib, home is home after all.'

Yes, home was home, but Zaib had spent almost twenty years of her life in Zakar, her entire youth and it had left its mark. Zakar's charm lay in its beauty, its adorning sea, its Bedouin ruins and desert secrets, it was where she had become a woman, where she had met a man who would remain with her until she breathed her last, where she had given birth to her daughters. She associated the melancholic beauty of the desert with all the most important experiences of her adult life. Leaving Zakar now was like leaving a part of herself behind. But now was the time. Hassan knew things better, he was probably right.

For the next three months she thought of nothing but their move back home. Hassan left his job and cashed in all his savings. He had no job to go to in Lahore but with his experience he could even start his own consultancy firm. Zaib knew he could do it; he was bright and excellent at his job. They wondered if 'home' would be the same. They told the girls with trepidation. Alya seemed more excited about moving, Sonia complained about leaving her friends behind.

'Ammi, we are not going to live near Devi khala, are we?'

'No, I don't think so, she lives outside the city now. Why, I thought you loved it there.'

'Nothing, just that I don't want to live near *them*.'

'Ok, honey, we won't.' Zaib hugged Sonia tight.

The day they were leaving Zaib went to the dock where she took one last look at the boats, water birds locked to the sea, their mission and their majesty still a mystery to her. She blew a kiss to the sea and wished one day she could be a part of the ocean. That evening she told Hassan that when she died she wanted her body to be thrown in the sea, rather than be buried. He made his promise. It never did happen but she was happy that he had agreed, for now, and that's all that really mattered.

CSSO

Lahore was much the same as they had left it except that it seemed less welcoming when they were actually living there after so many years. They had to get used to the corruption, the lack of privacy, the pollution.

The girls hated their new school at first. Alya was angry. 'They act as if we are different because we have English accents.'

'Tell them, you speak the Queen's English and they'll wish they could.'

'Their accents are so working class anyway.'

Working class. Yes, the pathetic, hateful, despised working class. The working class people that swept their floors, cooked their food, ironed their clothes and bathed their children. The hateful working class. It saddened Zaib to hear her child speak like that.

Hassan was out of the house meeting one of his old college friends one afternoon. Zaib sat on the sofa, and switched on the television. The maid, Suraya had just finished sweeping the floor and was about to mop it with a wet cloth.

'Baaji, should I press you legs? You must be tired.'

'No Suraya I am fine, really, just check on the food for me, will you?'

That night Suraya was about to leave when she went to Zaib, 'Baaji can I have some chapatti to take home, I would be grateful. We don't have *atta* because my husband is out of a job again.'

'What did your husband do before?'

'He was a painter, he painted people's houses, but these days there is nothing, he has no work.'

A few days later she came and sat at Zaib's feet again and started pressing her legs.

'Baaji, my husband does *nasha.* He smokes that stuff and he drinks. He comes home late and when I say no to him he hits me. I have scars too.' She bared her right shoulder to show Zaib a purple bruise.

'Tell him to come and see me. You know if you want I can have him arrested.'

'No no baaji please you don't say anything to him, I am just telling you. If you talk to him he will hit me more.'

'Just bring him here, he won't hurt you again.'

The following week Suraya's husband was there, sober and thin.

'Do you work?'

'Yes baaji, when I can find work.' He barely looked up at her.

'You treat your family with *izzat* otherwise I will call the police, do you understand?'

'Oh no no baaji, they will beat me and do other things besides, I would rather die. I will do what you say baaji, I never do that baaji. Has my wife been lying to you?'

It had been a week and Suraya hadn't come to work. Zaib was worried. What if he had killed her? She enquired in the neighbourhood if anyone had seen her but no one could find her. Almost six months later she found someone who knew her. She was an old woman who used to collect garbage from the street Zaib lived in. Zaib had often stared at her white beard, which the old woman wore with such ease.

'Baaji, she went with another.'

'With another man?'

'Yes baaji, she was with him and that is why her husband beat her, she has left him. She is bad baaji, you don't want her now. She asked me if she could come back to you, I say no, baaji is respectable woman she will not take you back.'

'Where is her husband now?'

'He still follows her, but he was beaten up badly, now he is always drugged, you know, in *nasha* baaji, the needle. The needle, baaji, once you take it, you can't leave it, you know.'

She turned away, with the hundred-rupee note in her hand that Zaib had just given her; she started her walk, her frosted chin shining under the sunlight. Zaib wanted to touch it, just then, for one moment, but the woman's eyes were fixed on the road in front of her and she disappeared. Noora, a younger woman, also a garbage collector, commonly known as the '*kuray wali*' (dust-bin woman), walked past, a cigarette in her hand. She called out to her, '*Asalamwalikum* Noora, how are you?'

'*Theek hun* baaji, are you well?' She had one hand on her hip and a mischievous smile on her lips.

Noora lived life on her own terms and Zaib admired her for it. Her husband had died four years ago leaving her to bring up five children on her own, but Noora never complained: Noora smoked her cigarettes openly, she had lovers she flaunted openly. She had no qualms about talking frankly about her life to anyone and everyone who would care to listen and she often told Zaib stories about her latest lover and how much he doted on her. She said they all worshipped her.

Suraya came to see Zaib one Thursday. She told her she had suffered so much abuse from her husband that she finally ran away with another man and sent her husband the divorce papers. Zaib could never have guessed that she could be so courageous. It was unheard of in poorer communities for a woman to ask a man for divorce.

'Baaji you know I love this one, he takes care of me and the old one, well I hope he dies and goes to hell. I am happy now.'

Suraya had risked her life for love. Zaib looked at her and smiled. That was true courage.

'So when are you coming back to work?'

The next day Suraya came back.

Zaib enjoyed the tenderness and care she got from Suraya and she looked forward to her daily visits.

ଔଷ

16

Dolls

Alya waited for the next sigh, a twitch, a movement from her mother. Anything that proved she was alive. Ammi wake up, wake up. It's me, Alya. She was suddenly struck by a mask she had stuck up on her wall as if she had never seen it before. A paper mache mask with red lips and huge black eyes. It took her back to ammi's porcelain dolls and her many masks. Had she been awake she would have commented on this mask. She would have liked it, possibly.

And then came the dolls. Doll dolls dolls. Dolls with multiple faces and glass eyes. Dolls that Alya now avoided at all cost. Ammi loved her 'perfect' porcelain dolls. Alya was running through the corridors of a department store in Lahore trying to find the sweets section. Zaib was chasing her.

'Alya stop it, will you! I can't keep running like this!'

After ammi had bought them copious amounts of sweets and lots of chocolates she had taken them to a toyshop nearby.

'Ammi, can we buy some toys too?' piped up Sonia.

'No darling no toys today. Ammi wants to buy something for herself for a change!'

Both girls followed her to the section where there were rows of porcelain dolls – Victorian, modern, some with frilly blue dresses and sparkling green eyes, others with huge billowing frocks and perfect hands and feet.

Ammi stared at them for several minutes looking at the minutest details of their clothes. She brushed her hands across their faces, their perfect upturned noses, their rosy cheeks, their tissue dresses. Alya recalled calling out to ammi but ammi couldn't hear her. Eventually she picked one with a white dress with several layers of frills and blue eyes. 'She is perfect'. Zaib placed her on her mantelpiece in her bedroom as soon as they arrived home. She spent some time adjusting her dress and then stood back and smiled with satisfaction.

'There, my room is now complete.' She looked into the doll's eyes and touched her cheek, 'You, my sweetheart will be called Amber. Just like the ocean sky.'

Alya had felt strangely jealous. During the next ten years Zaib collected a dozen more dolls at least. For each she had a name and sometimes she talked to them with a tender affection.

The girls tried not to visit their mother's room too often.

The dolls stared at Alya, lined up like an army ready for the kill.

'Ammi please wake up. Should I get Amber for you?'

ଓଃ

17

Victoria

Mummy used to say you should always treat servants with dignity but never be 'too nice' in case they got out of hand. She forgot to mention what would happen if the master or the mistress of the house got out of hand like Devi's husband had. He had slept with most of his maids because he thought it was his right to and he reveled in the power he had over them. He told a friend once, 'The pleasure you get from buying a woman is unequalled because you know they are merciless, you know they will do anything for you.' In her last conversation with Zaib, Devi was complaining that her maids were becoming condescending towards her because they knew they were his sexual preference. It made Zaib sick to think, Devi had accepted so much. It also made her sad; she wished she had spoken to Haider's mother herself that terrible day Devi's future was destroyed. She would have begged her for her sister's sake. Now this new pathetic Devi, who had succumbed to so much, was actually living in the same house as the women her husband was sleeping with. That same brilliant Devi who had come back from Oxford, full of hope and wonder. She could have touched the sky with those dreams. It seemed like yesterday. Zaib couldn't stop trying to erase Devi's new life in her mind.

Zaib asked her once, 'Don't you feel angry?'

'With whom?'

'The girls and HIM.'

'No, it's just the way he is, and they need the money, it's as simple as that.'

'What happens when he comes to you?'

'What do you mean? I am his wife. I have needs too. Besides what he has with me he doesn't have with them.'

Zaib had looked at her in disbelief. 'Devi that is immoral.'

'I think that's for me to decide. Plus I pray to my god and he listens, I know that.'

She couldn't bring her back anymore, she was lost to something far more powerful than Zaib could ever imagine.

Her mind wandered back to her home, her present in which Victoria often occupied her thoughts.

Victoria was employed to wash and iron the family's clothes every morning. She had black hair and a dusky complexion, large doe eyes and a slender figure. Her eyes shone with expectation. That was the best part for Zaib.

The winter had arrived and Zaib was thinking about her mother's Christmas tree. Every year she would put up a huge Christmas tree, which *had to be real*. She'd be running around with excitement calling her daughters, 'Tree trimming time! Come on girls. Who is going to put the angel at the top?' Now there was just silence and the tree was gone. So was mother and her voice.

Victoria came to her room. She said she was going to arrange a party in their *basti* and that Zaib and her family were invited. Zaib wished she could be there, if only just to watch for a while and catch a glimpse of their celebrations. If only to see the lights twinkle on the Christmas tree.

'Victoria, I'll try to come, but can't promise.'

The day of the Christmas party Zaib went in the car to the *basti* to drop Victoria home.

'Bibi, please come in and have a cup of tea.'

She longed to go in, but was scared of Hassan and the others, what would they say if they found out? She felt the eyes of her driver on her back scrutinizing her. *So she does have Christian blood in her,* they were saying. She wanted to spit in his face. She wanted to go in just to spite him. The multi-coloured lights on someone's Christmas tree winked at her through a window as she drove past the window. When she came home the world was still and dark like the bark of a tree before the rain and she felt empty. Hassan arrived from work, tired. The girls were complaining about their homework. Zaib stood apart in a world of her own.

'Zaib are you alright?' It was Hassan's voice.

'I want to celebrate Christmas.'

'Christmas is tomorrow.'

'I know, can't we get a tree today?'

'Zaib, we have already discussed this.'

'No, we have not. You have told me what to do, that is not a discussion.'

'People will talk, the girls will suffer. Things haven't changed here. You know I have no problems with it Zaib.'

'You are such a small person Hassan. It's because of the apathy of people like you that things DON'T change!'

'Whatever. But I will not have my girls explaining themselves to people.'

There was no tree.

Zaib was the matchstick girl.

Another conversation.

The phone interrupted them. It was Alya. She was asking Zaib to pick her up from a party.

Zaib put the phone down and turned to Hassan, 'She is in love you know.'

'Who?'

'The next-door neighbour! Alya of course, can't you see her mooning and staring into thin air all the time!'

'She is? With whom?' He looked worried.

'Sohail, a boy in school.'

'She is far too young for all this.'

'She is sixteen. Do you remember someone was only eighteen when she got married? Besides he is very good looking, she has good taste.'

He looked at her disapprovingly.

That night Hassan hardly spoke to Alya. Allowing her to grow up was a frightening prospect for a father. She guessed he might know something and worried that if he knew he might think less of her. She ate her dinner slowly.

Zaib looked at Victoria. She felt an ache in her stomach. She wondered what Victoria thought of her. Did she notice her at all? Couldn't Victoria acknowledge her in any way, just so she knew she mattered? Victoria did her job meticulously and with passion. She didn't care about the world outside her own, a world she could not see. While Victoria waited for the clothes to soak in the soapy water, she stood up straight arching her back, with her hands on her hips, her feet a foot apart, staring at the clothes in the bucket. She looked thoughtful and slightly impatient at the same time, and then started scrubbing, with her right hand, in wave like motions. She had pulled her *shalwar* up to make herself more comfortable and to make sure it would remain as dry as possible and sat on a small cane *peeri* with her legs wide apart. Zaib could see the muscles of her arms contract as she scrubbed harder. Zaib was amazed at the fluidity of her movements. Even the simple act of pulling her *shalwar* up and tucking it in to the sides of her waist, was done with so much grace and dignity, so much purpose. She raised her hands to roll her braided hair into a bun as the sun shone on her face. She was irresistible; she affirmed life. Victoria saw her looking at her.

'Baaji what are you doing out here? It is very hot. Go inside.' It was an order.

She was flustered. 'Yes Victoria you are right I am going in.'

Victoria had a manner that convinced others she was usually right. She worked at three different houses in the mornings before she came to Zaib's house. One was the house of an old woman, who was lonely and generally remained irritable and abusive. Victoria told Zaib about an incident once when she had forgotten to sweep the veranda and the old woman made her clean it four times in one day. Then there was the other time when she was washing the floor of the balcony and the old woman told her she was wasting time and wanted to stay up there as long as possible to flirt with the neighbours' sons. 'You know Zaib bibi, she said to me, "You are just a *badmash* who needs a man all the time." Then she added, "these Christians can't get enough of it. Damn them and their dirty blood."'

'Why don't you leave her for God's sake and try and find another house? You shouldn't have to hear such abuse from anyone!'

'Bibi you know it's so difficult to get good jobs these days, I have to look after my family and this is better than having no food in the house. My sisters and brothers have to go to school too.'

'Do you like anyone, any boy?' Zaib asked her once while watching her hang the clothes out to dry.

'No bibi. We are not allowed,' Victoria said in a matter of fact manner.

'Don't you want to choose your husband yourself?'

'No bibi, who would know better than my parents, they knew me before I was even born!'

Zaib thought of her father's warning about Hassan, before he died, *He won't always be like this Zaib.*

Everyone changes daddy. Yes, daddy everyone does. He was right, Hassan had changed. But why? Was that just how life unfolds, do you merely become a reflection of your influences, your trials, or is there more to it, surely there is more to it.

'Yes, but what if they are wrong?'

She longed for Victoria's head on her lap. She wanted to feel her soft hair between her fingers.

'No bibi, not possible, parents always know what is best for their children.'

She admired Victoria's faith.

'You know bibi, it's a secret so please you don't tell anyone, but soon I will get married.'

Zaib's heart sank.

'Oh, so you are engaged.' There was a dull ache in Zaib's chest.

'Congratulations. So, who is he?' Her voice faltered.

'My cousin. He has a big house in the village and a lot of land in his name. Then I will just look after my house and not have to work ever again. We will have our own cow and chickens!' Her chest was jutting out as she stood there with her hands on her hips imaging her soon-to-be new life.

So Victoria was leaving her, happy and ready for her life, full of surprises. 'Baaji, of course I will come and visit.' It was as if she had sensed Zaib's fear. Zaib felt isolated once again, abandoned.

After Victoria had gone, Zaib often thought of that day she had watched her wash the clothes, when she epitomized all that was beautiful in life. In those fifteen minutes Zaib had covered a lifetime of love, with Victoria beside her. Zaib would close her eyes tightly with Hassan lying by her side at night, thinking of Victoria, of how much purpose she had given her. She stretched the moment of its creation to its limits.

☙❧

18

Dead Dreams

There was a knock on the door. It was Devi. Her hands covered with thick blue veins, her large eyes sad with anguish.

'How bad is it? Does she remember anything?' she asked Alya.

Perhaps it was better if Zaib didn't remember anything. Why was everyone so adamant to make her remember?

'I don't know she is still asleep and I tried Dr Rizwi but he is out of town until tomorrow. I don't know what to do when she wakes up. She is sleeping right now.'

Devi walked into the bedroom and brushed her hand across her sister's forehead. She recalled that dreaded phone call six years ago.

A small voice at the other end of the receiver had said, 'Khala, it's me, Sonia. Abba has gone.'

Gone? Where? Despite all that had transpired between them Devi knew Hassan adored Zaib. He couldn't have left her just like that.

'What do you mean gone? Gone where?'

'We don't know, but he's gone. His things have gone and when ammi wakes up she will die. Please do something.'

Sonia sounded frantic which wasn't like her.

Devi had gone over straight away. Zaib was still delirious from the previous night. She was running from room to room, 'Hassan! Hassan, where are you?' 'Hassan I need to talk to you.'

Now she will die, thought Devi. Devi had seen the first signs of trouble about a year after they had arrived in Pakistan. She was visiting her sister. She had opened the cupboard to get Zaib her tweezers, when she saw a bottle of vodka next to her make up.

'What is this doing here?' she had asked Zaib.

Zaib didn't look at her in the eye, 'Oh Hassan must have left it there by mistake, we had some people over last night.'

In the evening when Hassan came back from work, Devi was still there. After meeting Devi he had turned to Zaib, 'Zaib, by the way where is that bottle of vodka I had in my cupboard? Better give it to me so I can lock it up, you know the servants might start taking swigs out of it!'

Zaib didn't look at her sister.

More and more often Devi could smell alcohol on Zaib's breath, but she was too terrified to confront her. One day she could no longer contain herself. 'Zaib, why are you drinking at ten in the morning?'

'Oh it's just a small drink, can't hurt me.'

'Zaib it's not good for you.'

'Devi, please let's not make a big deal out of it, it relaxes me, there's nothing wrong with that.'

That's when she had realized there was a problem. Within months it had got worse and for the first time Devi saw Hassan look helpless…

Zaib had started drinking small quantities of wine in Zakar at cocktail parties and boring get-togethers where people smiled away their pasts and said things they didn't mean. The wine dulled her senses enough to be able to bear their incessant chatter. She had never been a part of these elitist gatherings; in fact she hated them with venom. These were the kind of people responsible for the misery her father suffered in his last years, they had cut him off, severed all ties with him, made him feel like he had fallen from grace, shamed him when he needed them the most. These were the kind of people who said things like, 'You must be careful about your servants, they are not like us, they can be vicious and they will stab you in the back whenever they get a chance.' Stab people like you, thought Zaib, when she heard someone saying that at a ladies' tea party she had been forced to attend. If they weren't complaining about their servants they were discussing the latest fashions and the jewellery they had bought, the mindless, banal lot that they were, each living in her own cocoon, in her cotton-wool house propped up by opulent furnishings and well dressed children. Their hands shone with diamonds as they gesticulated wildly when they spoke and their eyes had a devilish glint in them with the knowledge that they could destroy anyone's life with a few choice words; after all they were the privileged lot who decided who was worth meeting and who wasn't; they wrote the biographies of people who they barely knew. They were the ones who had *the power.*

Zaib made sure she could find her way outside them and their cruelties with the help of her wine. In Pakistan it was illegal for Muslims to buy alcohol but she still managed to buy it in the black market. It was expensive but Hassan had saved enough money in Zakar to last a while or at least until his business kicked off in Lahore. The first time Sonia saw mama drunk she cried all night. She didn't speak to her for two days. Zaib begged her to forgive her and promised it would never happen again. A few months later Sonia saw ammi drunk again. Then one day she heard ammi and abba fighting in the bedroom, ammi was drunk yet again. She was screaming, but her words were sometimes incoherent.

'You don't want to have sex with me because you think I am dirty!'

'I don't want to have sex with a drunk!'

She broke something and he left the room. Similar episodes became more and more frequent. Hassan stayed out for longer everyday and whereas Zaib previously used to wake up at eight every morning, she now stayed in bed until twelve or one.

Christmas was one day away and the girls were out with friends. They came home in the evening. At that time in the evening abba was usually still at work and ammi was at home reading or watching the television. That day she was in her room and the door was locked. Alya knocked several times but there was no response. Sonia called Suraya, who was crying. When she saw the girls her cry turned into a wail.

'Oh bibi bibi, where were you both?'

The smell of death filled Alya's head, they stood there unable to move. Alya thought she was going to die as the horror of hell passed through her.

'Your mother is ill, she is hurt! Oh bibi, please do something.'

Sonia's legs were failing her, but she stood calm.

Alya ran to her mother's bedroom. She tried to bang on the door with her fists, 'find the key, the key please someone!'

'Bibi it's not locked, push harder, she's probably put something against it.'

She pushed hard and almost fell into the room as the door burst open. 'Ammi please, ammi get up!' She shook her with all her strength. Still there was no reply.

'Call someone, what's wrong with her!'

Zaib was a small bundle of flesh and bones that lay still in a corner of the bed.

Sonia couldn't touch her. Alya waited to see if she was breathing. 'Ammi?' she whispered. The curtains were drawn, only a muddy light filtered through it. She finally turned her mother around and saw her grey face.

'Oh God, what's wrong?'

She had taken an overdose of sleeping pills. They rang their father. After a stomach wash and a lecture from the doctors in the hospital they came back. At least she was alive, at least they still had her. Sonia squeezed her father's arm affectionately. He hugged her, 'It will be ok, it will be, honestly.' Alya looked at him accusingly, 'What is happening to her?' It was all happening so suddenly. It was as if one day she was sane and the next she had gone. *What was really happening to her?* They all kept asking themselves the same question. And why? 'Don't you love ammi anymore?' was Alya's next question.

Hassan looked at her, shocked. Love was a small word for what he felt for Zaib. When he had married her he could never have imagined seeing her like this, a mere wisp of what she once was, yes he did love her, that was the least of what he felt for her Where had it all gone wrong and when? As these questions raced through his daughters' minds, so did they his, but it was of no use; there is no beginning or end to such questions. What happens between two people who share a bed, who share their lives, what breaks down between them and what is salvaged, is unknown, least by the two people themselves. Who knew what it really was. All that they could be certain of was what they saw, what they experienced, what they felt and the next few years were a test of their love, of their patience and above all else, of their faith.

His answer came after a pause, 'I don't know what to do.' His helplessness crushed her.

The next morning they went to check on ammi. She was fast asleep. Alya left to get dressed and Sonia stayed for a while watching her mother. She remembered herself climbing on ammi's back as a child and pestering her to tell a story.

'Which one?'

'The one about the three bears and the girl with golden hair.'

Ammi was always ready to tell them stories when they were children. Once they had heard all the fairy tales in the books, she made them up. She made up names of fairies and painted their world with the most exquisite images and scenes of emerald forests whispering tales of love and happiness. Even at fourteen, Sonia sometimes asked mummy to tell her a story. How sad ammi looked now, lying in bed, frail and disappointed, thought Alya. Where did all the wonder go? Was she dreaming of her fairies and pixies now? Was she in wonderland with daddy? She noticed a slight frown on her forehead. Maybe she was having a nightmare; maybe daddy was leaving her. That was Sonia's greatest fear. What would she do if abba left her? She'd die. She needed him so much, then why was she pushing him away, cutting him out. Sonia had tried to ask her mother many times, but Zaib had simply denied that anything was wrong as if she were living in some dream world.

'Ammi, why are you and daddy fighting all the time?'

'We are not. All couples fight.'

'Are you blind, ammi? They don't fight like you.'

'Stop being paranoid sweetheart.' She would pinch her cheek when she had something to hide.

Soon Zaib started forgetting things and the girls thought maybe she was losing her mind.

⁂

Hassan is on his way to London on a business trip where he will meet lots of suits and encounter umpteen grey streets with earlobe signs telling him there is always a plan. The plane is still on the ground and the runway has been licked clean several times (he cannot see the small imperfections, but he leans forward hoping he might so that he can be saved somehow before the plane takes off). He is looking frail and tired. (Some of her winking glitter is still on my hands... though I washed it off a long time ago). People look nervous for some reason and a porcelain air-hostess smiles. These people are all in unison, and Hassan is looking on, maybe they are magicians and Hassan knows nothing, maybe he knows nothing of what's really happening. *I wish I could get out of this* ... He is trapped in his seat. He is trying to listen to the words but he can't, he is forced to listen to the engine drilling into him ... he wants to go back to where he can't even remember... before mother and father, before what he has known. There is much interference now while I am trying to tell you ... *and them*. There is interference from the ghosts in his genes and there is interference from the roses in the garden where the water from the tap is connected to a hose ready to burst into a fountain. And ... there are peaches on a tree we are not allowed to touch. Hassan sees his mother wearing a white *kurta*: she is smiling at her best friend who is wearing a pink *dupatta,* a pink cloud in a haze. His mother's face is brown shining Vaseline soft and her lips tend to stick together when she talks just as they used to when she was alive. He is trying to hear what she is saying but he is too far away to catch her words and he feels frustrated. He wishes he could be with her now, wrapped inside her arms, hidden.

When he arrives in London the stinging cold air clears his head. He sees Zaib standing at the top of a mountain clapping her hands and calling out to him 'Daddy daddy come catch me!' He runs towards her.... They have played songs on trembling leaves together and touched the felt tip mildew on mountain lakes. They have danced to the cadence of their rugged surroundings knowing that array of thoughts, ideas are multiplying always, creating, obliterating and sometimes like the sphinx uncertain and without an end; still it didn't matter to them, they were in love.

Now he can hear the spoon in his cup stirring continuously, round and round; the cruel circle fixed in its resolve to carry on in a frightening time when Zaib smiles and talks incessantly about daddy, *her Hassan*.

☙❧

19

Dirt

Alya looked at her sleeping mother and felt dirty once again. My poor ammi.

'Alya go and clean up now. Come on good girl.' Again she went back to the first time Asad had had sex with her. It was as if it had just happened, but for some reason the small details kept changing and it disconcerted her. She wanted to preserve the memory and try and remember it 'as it was'. It was maddening. She went through it again. Again, again, again to get it right – to get it right in her mind.

He kissed her lips and started fondling her small hard breasts with his palms, playing with her nipples with his fingers. When he touched her erect nipples she felt a rush of liquid fill up between her legs. He cupped her vagina with his hand and started stroking her, as he pulled gently on her soft pubic hair. She arched her back and moaned with pleasure and within seconds he was lying on top of her. Somehow her legs had automatically opened, as if of their own free will and he placed his penis on her vagina and began pushing. As he pushed harder she felt a searing pain and tried to push him off. 'Please stop! Stop, it's hurting me!' He covered her mouth with his hand and whispered 'Shsh shsh it will be fine in a moment – you'll see you will enjoy it.' His body felt like bricks on her. She was pinned to the bed. I am suffocating! The pain, the pain was so sharp, she could still feel the pain, a knife slicing her. Her screams were muffled by his hand. Please let me scream! Would it never end? Please please, Asad bhai stop! When it was over he got up and threw a sheet on her. 'Are you ok? You know I love you Alya. This time maybe it wasn't so good for you, but next time you will really enjoy it. Go and clean up now.' He patted her on the head. She had no idea she was bleeding. When she stood up a stream of blood trickled down her thighs. Initially, she felt scared but looking at Asad sitting next to her, she was reassured. In the bathroom she washed herself thoroughly and wiped herself with a towel. When she came back Asad was smoking a cigarette. 'I will get you something from the chemist so that you can put it in your underwear. It will absorb the blood. It shouldn't take more than a day or so for your body to adjust.'

The next day they sneaked out of their rooms at night when everyone was sleeping. The pain was less this time and she enjoyed it a little. Slowly, she started to look forward to their 'sessions' as he called them. Every time after that she couldn't wait to feel him inside her and fantasized about it constantly. One day he said he didn't feel like it.

She insisted. 'Please Asad bhai. I just want to feel you. Just once.'

He had slapped her. 'Haven't you had enough?'

The tears rolled down her face involuntarily.

A few minutes later he had taken her into his arms, 'I am sorry. I don't know why I just can't do it right now. Please forgive me.'

The next time they experimented with different positions. 'Today I will take you from the back.' Every time they had sex, they tried new positions and postures. Sometimes when she was on her knees she'd get carpet burns and her knees would hurt for days but he told her she should be proud of the burns as they were a sign that they had had good wild sex. Other times she'd notice bruises on her thighs from where he had been holding on to her while he put it inside her from the back. Sex became like a drug for them and they couldn't wait to explore strange new worlds together. The elation she felt was unequalled and she mapped out her life with Asad. 'Asad bhai we will get married, won't we?'

'My darling I can't imagine one day without you.'

They were the most beautiful words she had heard.

On days when Asad was feeling particularly unhappy she would assuage him by taking care of his needs and telling him over and over again how much she loved him. Now when she thought about it she was transported back to that time and sometimes she wished it had never ended. She would never again feel that passion, that sense of worth.

With him she was sheltered from ammi, her father, even Sonia. She told herself so many times how wrong it was, but then his words echoed in her head, 'Alya you were born a woman. You were meant to be with me.' Maybe it was the right time for her.

When she finally left Asad years later, she craved for him for a while. When the family moved back to Pakistan she started seeing several men of different ages, sometimes sleeping with them within hours of knowing them. Her appetite for sex was insatiable and she fantasized about sex all the time. Somehow none of them measured up to Asad but she was compelled to try and find 'the right one' and until that moment came she kept having sex with one man after another. She began to use them for their bodies and hated them after it was over. She had sex with brothers at the same time, best friends, even lovers and betrayed them whenever she got fed up. She enjoyed the betrayal because it made her feel more in control, more powerful. On days when she was alone, she would wash herself several times in the bath, scrubbing her hands, her face, her thighs to clean herself properly. When she'd come out she would want to smell sex on her again. One afternoon she had just come home after meeting her boyfriend. She had had sex with him four times that day. Zaib thought she was spending a day with a friend of hers who was covering for her.

'How was your day?' Zaib asked her as she walked into her room.

'Good. Fine. I'm just a little tired.'

'Well, get something inside you. You are looking too thin these days.'

She remembered thinking, is that all you have to say? Don't you know? Don't you know anything outside yourself? She was so fed up of it all. And then she was dirty again. Dirty dirty dirty.

Hanging, hanging, hanging, upside down, where you see me inside me shsh shsh shsh... he will cut me open and eat me inside out... he loves my flesh and I can feel him inside me cradling my womb in his hands... baby baby baby, I will lick myself clean clean clean... me me me his baby in his arms asad asad asad love me. He is in me now, asad?

ଓଃ

20

Faith

'Devi khala, can you please tell me what to do? I don't know what she will be like when she wakes up.' Alya paced the room.

Devi was deep in thought. 'Can we try and contact Brian? He is the only link to that place. Maybe he can help us.'

'Let's contact the British Council in Zakar, they'll be able to give us some leads.'

They rang the British Council in Zakar.

A woman answered: 'Yes, we have a Brian Benning listed here, he worked here more than ten years ago. I am afraid we don't have an address but luckily we have a number. It's the number of his home in Britain.'

Alya dialed the number. A man answered, 'Yes?'

'I am the daughter of an old friend of Brian's, can I speak to him?'

ꕥ

All those years ago in Zakar, Brian had left suddenly to teach English as a foreign language in Beijing. He had told Zaib it was his only chance to see China and he didn't want to miss it. He was to return six months later. Zaib had missed him and wished she too could somehow have gone with him just for a while. When he came back she couldn't contain her happiness. The minute she saw him she felt such an immense surge of emotion she wanted to jump into his arms, hold him, kiss him, be with him forever, she tried to take it all in with one brief look. His smile was gentler now. He stood still and stared at her with affection, his arms wide open, 'It's so good to see you Zaib.'

He held her tight. She put her head on his shoulder and then he kissed her on her lips. She looked at him, her eyes moistened and then she withdrew, 'I love you Brian, but I can't, do you understand? I am sorry.'

He released her. 'I understand. I am sorry Zaib.'

Brian and Zaib met only once more. He was part of a sin she could not face. The only time she saw Brian again, she didn't say much. She knew she had to let him go before it was too late.

As for Brian, in that interlude from life's maddening indifference, he had found a joy he never lost, and it sheltered him for the rest of his years. Eventually, he left her with no sign of where he was going. He was altered after he left; though she remained a part of him, there was nothing he could do but relinquish himself to the measured existence most of us do when we have few dreams worth pursuing and only memories to remind us what we could have had or been. Years later when Brian was on his deathbed, he spoke of her.... of the time they had together and of a wish he had to have seen her just once more... would she have known that at that moment he was calling out to her one last time? Would she have known that Brian was long gone, long before she breathed her last. But it had to be done, the way it was, not in any other way just as it was, intact, frozen in history. It was a trial of many lives intertwined with each other, determined by one stroke of the brush, with no beginning and a beautifully uncertain purpose. They, the players, lived in the continuum of that time and that love.

'Can I speak to Brian please?'

'I am afraid you can't. He died of pneumonia two years ago.'

❧

Zaib had always been troubled by questions about religion, class and creed. She wanted answers, answers that were just not there. In her bed, on days when she felt particularly vulnerable, she thought about such questions, but inevitably failed to reach a resolution. Were all religions as Marx said just an opiate of the masses? Can they be written off that easily? Or was life really just a series of tests? Were we being judged according to our actions? Then how could actions be judged? If actions should be judged as right or wrong then it followed that motives must surely be judged as well because an action is not possible without motive. Motive is based on a series of events that could be given a number or even known, simply because they were a thought process. A thought process was by its nature unknowable and often irrational, therefore motive could never be known precisely, and so it followed that people could only judge actions by actions themselves. What makes those actions right or wrong was the view of the collective public. So human beings adhered to a public law, which determined right and wrong, moral or immoral. Where did religion fit in then? Wasn't religion the point where the argument started? Then how did she drift so far away from it? Was it in that grey area, the unknown black holes people know nothing about? Was it that *x* factor everyone secretly believed in? So it was more than just a public language called upon for judgement, it was really about common *concepts*. The concept of red, for example, was similar for everyone even if the word was different in different languages. It was when there was a conflict between concept and language that human explanation failed. Humans were then left with a multitude of questions that man and logic could not answer. There was no shame for Zaib in following the rule of religion just as there was no shame in following the rule of man. The only shame that kills one, she thought, was the shame of not being able to follow your own rules. And she had failed.

Over the years Zaib had become less forgiving of herself and more fearful of God. She didn't pray or follow scripture; she just *knew* that certain things were true. She believed in sin. She recognized the change in herself and wondered why she felt so shattered. Why had Hassan changed she thought? He was the same daddy then why did she feel so lonely? He just seemed so aloof and uninterested in her now. She couldn't think of how to make him look at her the way he used to. She had said it to him many times, 'Daddy why don't you look at me with *that look* any more?' 'What look?' 'You know, like you adore me and like I fascinate you all the time.' All he said was that he had grown out of being that expressive and that his love was evident in other ways. What other ways could there be, she wondered.

She could have slept and woken up a million times a day, the difference between one state of consciousness and another could barely be deciphered. Days merged into one another and the nights were painful premonitions of the day to come. After that day with Brian, she felt guilty and cheated at the same time. Maybe if Hassan had given her more attention she wouldn't have felt so intensely attracted to Brain, so close to giving in to him. But more than anything else she was ashamed, she had betrayed herself. She started thinking of ways to hurt herself. The children would be fine without her; they seemed to care about their father more anyway. Death seemed like a peaceful escape. She had also become more fearful of the idea of an afterlife. Her dread grew everyday, ... it's your actions in this life that count for the next, they are your gateway to a better place, this is the first act of many, it's just the prologue. Is all this even real? thought Zaib one day. Oh if only Brian was here, he'd understand. She had lost her old Brian, her best friend to an act of dishonesty, her 'dishonesty and his weakness'.

She looked for Brian again, wise and kind.

Zaib's roses had spread like a blanket, looking for new lives and new crows chatting on side streets with butterflies for crowns.

Matchstickmen could never understand the truth about Brian and what he meant to her. She had beads of perspiration on her forehead, she could have sunk into the ground, but to an onlooker she was just looking out of her window, focusing on one invisible spot in the garden.

There was a shuffle at the door. Zaib continued to look out of the window. It was Sonia, 'Ammi, I was wondering can we go for a holiday to Pakistan? I really love it there.'

She looked at her daughter thoughtfully, 'It's too late honey, too late now.'

ଔ

The schools were closed for the summer, leather heat stuck to their skins. Alya and Sonia often stayed up talking late at night, their hilarity tickling the air around them, their voices, dust. Zaib listened to them from her room, lovingly, enviously. They reminded her of herself and Devi when they were girls. Those girls no longer existed; they had been obliterated from the face of the earth, even the thought of them stung. And then there was daddy, her Hassan. He was never there anymore. He would often come home after she and the girls had eaten dinner. That is when she felt like eating dinner.

She and Hassan were barely communicating any more unless she was drunk.

She asked him again and again, 'Daddy I wait all day just for a hug. Pleeeease daddy give me a hug.'

'I am tired Zaib. I just don't feel like it right now? That doesn't mean I don't love you. Things change.'

Not for me. Things don't change with daddy. This time, neither Devi, nor her father were there to help her. Quietness spreads like ink between people and that means they do anything to escape the dread of each other's thoughts, each other's questions, but Hassan's feelings of desolation spread through his days and Zaib could see it. She suggested they use some of their savings in Zakar to take a holiday and travel the world without the girls. There was a sudden panic in Hassan's eyes. He just looked anxious and she dwelled on it until the room was bleeding with crows. What was he really thinking about? Why did he seem hesitant? Was being with her that unbearable to him? Was there someone else? Her eyes circled various objects in the room making them into shapes and insects, cutting them out of the room and the walls, until she wanted to tear her mind out. Daddy you do love me don't you? He came home late from work that night looking harassed and trapped. Why was he late? So Hassan, what happened? What happened to us? Daddy? He looked anxious again.

Which day should I pick to step on a life? Will it make a difference whether it's Sunday or Saturday, July or June, sunny or cold… The salt breeze of Zakar's beaches washed over her face.

❧

21

Papermen

They called him a rotten apple because he hated studying. After the sleeping pills and Irum, Asad was ostracized from society. The parents of his school friends were especially vocal on his many faults and they dissuaded their children from meeting him as he was considered a *bad* influence. In the end Asad never amounted to much in the eyes of the world. In the eyes of his father he was a disappointment and in the eyes of his mother, an angel. For him it was much the same thing.

Asad went to an all-boys school. His school was known to be one of the best in the country. A leftover from the British Raj in India, the school, was known for its excellent academic record and its highly qualified teachers who frequently caned the children until they laughed when they were being caned and cried at night in bed when their hands and heads hurt. The parents usually ignored this aspect of the school because it was so well known and had such big names attached to it. Asad's father insisted on sending both his sons there because it was so 'reputable' and had such big names attached to it. Asad and his brother mostly ended up feeling inadequate. They couldn't compete with their rich friends who took them for car rides and expensive meals in fancy restaurants. Asad remembered one of them asking him what material his shirt was made of, 'Who cares, I like it,' was his answer. 'I only wear pure cotton in the summer.' And then he lied, 'It's Armani.' His brother, Bilal was stronger and he found an escape for himself by studying as hard as he could so he could get out to of the country to study abroad. He was going to try for a scholarship, which he eventually got and went to do Mathematics at university in Colorado. He never came back. Asad, however, would come home from school looking miserable and make plasticine figures, plasticine cars, plasticine houses and fill his room with plasticine in different colours. He drowned in his world of plasticine and woke up only to eat...

Plasticine broccoli head pulsates. It's circular – the pink and blue men collapsing in his hands. I peeped inside to see how they swayed in his hands. Plasticine piano, plasticine men on table tops grinning together ... On Sunday I saw muddy footpaths grow into massive mountains with fir trees balancing like ballerinas on their slopes, sweeping the ground slowly and gathering prism conversations of men and sullied sounds of people baking pancakes on bright blue days, sometimes splashed with yellow red and green. I don't know what he is doing but listening and scratching a tree with a twig, staring at one point in the ground as if he has seen a miracle. I can't see the miracle from here but it's there. He is scooping up his vomit with his hands before big people see it and waiting for his girl friend to come and hug him before it's time for her to hide away from him. It is only now, after being inside his head that I know he and everybody else in the world are actually angels.

When news of Asad's suicide attempt reached Zaib, she flew home immediately. Devi was there at the airport with arms outstretched and the same big sad moon-eyes. But this time, there was something in her eyes that old Zaib, she was going to be strong. For the first time Zaib saw a resolve in her, a determination she hadn't seen since she was in her teens. She told Zaib he would be all right. 'Thank God he is alive Zaib.'

What had her sister done to deserve this? She remembered her nephew's habits as a baby, the way he would put his little arms around his mother whenever he sensed she was upset, the way he would insist on climbing on top of Zaib's head and pull her hair and then wait for her to throw him off and tickle him until tears rolled down his cheeks. She could smell his baby lotion tummy and his chubby, powdered thighs. He used to be loving, bright and inquisitive. She recalled the times his father had degraded and demoralized Asad in front of her and if he was doing it so many times during Zaib's short visits to Pakistan, it must have been much worse when she wasn't there.

She remembered a particular day when he was furious with Asad because he had taken the car out for a drive and had come back late at night. The boy was seventeen. She kept going over her nephew's face, his dark enquiring eyes, his Peter Pan ears and busy hands. He was such an intelligent boy; he could have done so much in life. What had happened to the boy, to make him feel that there was no other way out? She didn't know how bad it really was. Devi had not told her about Irum. She couldn't figure it out. There was something missing.

That night in the hospital, she was surrounded by sickness. He was lying there, ashamed at having failed. 'Why didn't I just die?' he said. She was sitting near him, smelling the dying and their diseases surrounding them. She looked at his frail body, his weak hands. The pain in his head was constant. He told Zaib he didn't regret what he had done. She held his hand. 'Please beta, don't do it to us…' What do they know, he thought.

He had to tell her, if he didn't tell her he would never have the courage to do it again and he had to do it. In their mutual silence Zaib knew something was going to happen, just as she knew the day mummy told her Ghazala had died; again, today, she could do nothing but wait for it.

'Khala you mustn't be shocked about it, but please don't tell ammi.'

'Khala, do you know why I didn't want to study in an all-boys' school? Abba still forced me.'

Zaib remembered Devi telling her that Asad was unhappy in his school but her husband insisted that he carry on there. So he was forced to go to the same school until he had finished his A Levels.

'Auntie, the boys forced themselves on me. They were ruthless and frustrated bastards. Apart from the pain, of course. It wasn't easy after that.'

He looked at his hands. A sea of emptiness lay sprawled in front of them.

She held on to the side of his hospital bed. Her feet were sweating. She was in the middle of a white hospital room with a world outside that she had left behind, shut out of herself. This stark room was her present, her future, locking her inside it. Asad's cardboard sheets sniffed her hands.

He paused and then continued, 'There were five of them and they said it was a punishment for doing badly in my exams. After that they punished me again and again. I told Irum everything and she still chose *abba* and not me.'

She stayed for a while and then left. Later that day she had asked about Irum. Devi only told her the part about Irum being a drug addict, the rest of it she knew from what Asad had said. On the flight back all she could see was Asad's small face slowly disintegrating.

Bits of paper. Paper head. Paper man, Paper boys. They swing on puppet strings paper people, paper children paper arms paper legs paper eyes, paper eyes, sliding paper, flying. White paper snowflakes shifting places up and down up and down up an down reclining and sad tinsel thread....

❧

'Ammi, why don't we fall off the world?' Alya had a lot of questions like her mother once had when she was a child.

'We can't honey, the world is round.'

'Don't be silly ammi, the world is square and if I walk long enough I will fall off and go to another world.'

And like her father Zaib answered her questions patiently. But now she felt abandoned. Who would answer her questions, who could she lean on, ask for support? Abba was out all the time now and when he came home he looked distracted. The girls thought maybe it was all their fault. When he was home he would put his arms around them or give them a peck on the cheek and then turn away as if trying to hide something.

The house breathed new words and sounds. Deafening shadows washed the rooms repeatedly waking the girls up night after night....

The sour smell of wine muzzles Hassan just when he is about to speak. He can't make conversation, especially when they are celebrating something because that means she drinks even more and even the thought of talking makes him sick. She drinks everyday now. Today Hassan and Zaib are celebrating their eighteenth wedding anniversary. He is developing a fear of her shaking hands and morning nausea. He will take these to death with him. Zaib is celebrating their wedding anniversary with wine and olives. Hassan is in the room but he doesn't join her. He is sitting in front of her, thinking of something to say. She keeps smiling at him nervously and he detects a small pink twitch that wasn't there before, it is located just above her upper lip on the right side of her mouth. It becomes the focus of her face and Hassan thinks that if he doesn't walk away he will die of claustrophobia. He has to go before he is eaten up and thrown out like dog bones. After a few interminable minutes, he longs to get up, but her moving lips pin him down. He is fixed to the sofa.

'Daddy, please have some wine with me! Don't leave me today.'

After a moment, 'Are you sleeping with someone else?'

He looks her straight in the eye and she quickly looks away.

He can see himself in her exaggerated gestures. He must leave. He says he will be back after a short walk. He wonders if she can read him.

Outside, the cold, unsullied air, saddens him. His cheeks are marble and he is momentarily stunned by the fickleness of his body. He walks down his everyday street, littered with yesterday's newspapers and people's half-torn, empty, cigarette packets. He starts to think about Zaib. His feet are fluid. He isn't sure where he is, but it hardly matters anymore. He feels her eyes on him and the girlish innocence with which she questions him, settles on him uncomfortably. He holds her close to his chest and tells her all will be all right if she hugs him tight enough, but she doesn't believe him. She says she does, with all her heart and she tries to, but she doesn't believe him. That's when he tells her to close her eyes and picks her up from the collapsing earth. The ground is moist with dew and she is sinking into it quickly. She clutches on to his coat. While he is carrying her he looks at her closely. She is fascinating; he has never seen a more striking creature. She has hair like crooked twigs and knotty fingers with nails full of dirt and dust, and she smells like the first rays of dawn on a winter morning. He imagines her being his wife.

Five years later, she is his wife and she is watching television in their sitting room in Zakar. He wants to speak to her, but he wants her to say something first. He takes off his shoes and puts on his slippers. His feet feel hot. He is looking at her constantly from the bedroom. She is staring at the television, but he can see that she is not watching it. He walks into the sitting room and sits next to her, but she doesn't seem to notice. A few minutes pass and she looks around. 'Daddy, did you think I didn't see you watching me?' She jumps into his lap and starts giggling loudly. 'Daddy, daddy, daddy, I love you this much,' and she holds her arms out as wide as possible to show him how much. His body relaxes and he takes a sigh of relief.

Today is their anniversary. Zaib is home in her dollhouse. He hears her laughter but he doesn't see her. He wonders if it was all inevitable. He can smell red wine from the gutters on the streets of Lahore, he can smell it on his hands after he washes them in the sink and in the morning when he takes a shower. He thinks it's his fault. He recalls how his hands tremble when he removes the bed covers from their bed after he comes home from work. He wakes up shaking with demons in his head and spiders on his palms and he has imagined suffocating Zaib under the pillow many times. He cannot touch her body because he is frightened of its strength and its might but also of its tenderness, its fragility. They haven't made love for over six months. She wakes up in the middle of the night sometimes and asks him to make love to her, but he cannot because he fears her most of the time now.

One day she runs her fingers through his hair and tries to seduce him. He moves away because he cannot touch her alien body, so she starts screaming uncontrollably. He brings his legs up to the fetal position and lies still before suddenly getting up. He slaps her across the cheek and her cheek burns for some time, becoming pink like the twitch. She looks at him in disbelief and lies down in utter silence for the rest of the night. When the girls look at him strangely the next morning, as if they had seen him slapping their mother the previous night, he decides he doesn't want to see any of them again. He wants to run away and tell himself it's all a mistake. He comes home from work and Zaib is sleeping peacefully in her bed. The sheets cover her body lightly and Hassan kisses her forehead. He goes into the girls' room and asks them to make her mango milkshake because it's her favourite drink. He sits next to her and props her up with several pillows, holding the glass to her mouth, tilting it to a comfortable angle. She drinks it slowly, looking up at him and smiling every now and then, grateful for his love and oblivious of the previous day's pain. Then she says, 'You know daddy, I won't die in disgrace because you are with me.' And that's when he knows with an absolute certainty that he has to go.

He is defenceless.

He justifies his actions before leaving. Alya would never forgive him for failing her mother no matter what he did, Alya, his sweet sweet daughter, whom he adored more than she would ever know, was too far away from him now. He had to go because there were no reasons anymore, and nothing he could do. Would Sonia ever forgive him? He looks at Zaib and thinks how she is irretrievably altered. One by one he dissects them, Alya… Sonia… Zaib… and himself in relation to them and he knows he has lost his place in their lives. They are all a part of him, yet they have abandoned him. He can do nothing. Nothing. He opens Zaib's wardrobe and brushes his fingers across her clothes one last time. He breathes her and then he leaves She is with him on his short journey away from her.

☙❧

22

Curtain Call

Zaib was dreaming of Ghazala when she woke up by some strange sound in the house. Was there a difference between the real world and her dream world? Often she just didn't know. It became worse as her daughters grew older. She knew it was going to be hard, no matter how she spread herself in the middle of her two lives. She was looking down into her coffee cup and trying to see her reflection in the light-brown liquid.

That day when she woke up and realized Hassan wasn't home, she asked the servants where he was. Nobody had seen him all morning. She waited for Alya to come home from college.

She was sitting up in her bed, her toes making circles in the air. Alya felt something crawl up her leg: a gyrating fish.

'Alya you must know where your father is.'

She was so calm Alya thought something was wrong with her.

'I'm sure he'll be back soon. He often goes away for ages.'

'But his clothes are missing.'

Alya felt Asad inside her, her father's disappointed face, her inability to help her mother, inertia in her pulse, several emotions in seconds.

'Do you think he left because of me?'

She was a child. Her voice was meek.

'Of course not, ammi.'

Alya forgot herself for a minute and watched her mother dwindle. Zaib looked at her hands curiously as if she had never seen them before.

He had left, for ever, she knew it. She knew it so well. What would she do without him? Alya couldn't imagine her mother for one day without daddy. It seemed unnatural. She felt a chill in her bones, mice scuttled underneath her feet and Asad pushed her beyond her limits. Her legs were stiff with fear. She knew her father well. He wouldn't come back. What if they never saw him again? How would Zaib go on?

She tried to blame him. But hadn't he tried? She had seen him trying. What more could he have done?

She wondered where he had gone. Maybe, it *was* their fault. They were all partly responsible for his leaving. She had probably been such a difficult child that he was fed up, Sonia had been so indifferent recently and ammi had pushed it too far. When Sonia found out their father had left, she became morose and thoughtful for months, her mother and sister at the periphery of her world.

The day he had left Sonia had looked at Zaib's closed eyelids moving in her sleep. She examined the veins on them feeding her body, it made her shudder to think that she could just as easily stop breathing. She picked up her mother's limp, sleeping hand. One day, insects would eat *that* hand and crawl into the womb that had once held her in its shell. The whole thing seemed like a cosmic mistake. Was it possible for such a beautiful creature to be mutilated like that? The indignity of it astonished her. She defaced Zaib over and over again; it was the mental action of someone outside themselves making a reckless attempt to play the role of onlooker. It didn't help; instead it just made her realize how frugal nature had been in bestowing its creatures with pleasures and how generous it had been with its dreams. There was a continuous existing imbalance in everything she thought about and it caused a deathly panic in her. She looked at Zaib's face again. There she was, her perfect mother, negated by life and her husband; dead, with throbbing matrix functions only, and a sleeping smile that was her only reality right now. Still, she hoped something unexpected would happen. Maybe abba would come back.

Over the next few months the girls invented a million different ways to entertain their mother. They brought home her favourite movies, they bought songs she enjoyed listening to and made up jokes they thought she would find funny. They were determined to keep her alive somehow. Some days she was so uncooperative that they simply wanted her dead. They made plans for a mistake that would seem like an accident and would kill her instantly. Other days they hated themselves for letting such an idea come into their heads. As the months passed, everything felt stagnant. Whatever they did, Zaib just smiled, with a vague look in her eyes difficult to decipher. They caught fragments of realization, but nothing made sense. She kept thanking them for being such loving and caring daughters with a politeness that was exaggerated. They were alone and scared and there was nothing they could do.

One day Sonia asked her, 'Ammi,' she said, in a half whisper, 'should we call the police to find out where abba is?'

'If he doesn't want us anymore, let him go, let him fly fly fly!!' She was exaggerating her movements by flapping her hands like a bird.

Zaib began talking to her daughters about her life before she got married. She told them stories and how pretty their Devi khala used to be and how everyone in the (her mother's) family used to call her (Zaib) 'the one with the potato nose'. She didn't talk about Hassan at all and that worried them even more. She acted as if Hassan had never existed.

Hassan had left no physical trace of himself in the house. Where was he now? Perhaps trying to rid himself of the unspeakable, cleansing himself of his sores, or was he quietly reliving the agony of what he had had to endure in his last few years with Zaib.

For Zaib, in her moments of clarity, she told herself daddy had had enough.

My poor poor daddy. The mangoes have all been eaten now... Daddy's cancer had gone ... Ghazala told her she was in heaven.... she drank the cold air rising from the ground... and in the corners the ants were forming queues.

After weighing the options and considering every conceivable possibility, her daughters phoned one of Zaib's old college friends, Shabnam. She had known Zaib for years and had been visiting them quite often prior to Zaib's breakdown. Sonia spoke to her first.

'Auntie you know abba has left and we need some help with ammi.'

Shabnam told Sonia she was very sorry but she was too busy with a new project at work, which involved extensive travelling so she couldn't really help, but suggested they take their mother to a doctor. Alya phoned another friend, Afshan, who had always seemed sympathetic towards other people's troubles and who worked for a local nongovernment organization, counseling victims of child abuse. The girls were sure she would help.

She too refused.

'Auntie, please at least come and meet her, maybe she will feel better.' They hated talking about their mother like that, but the alternative was more terrifying.

'I am really sorry beta, you are so sweet and young, but you must consult a doctor.'

They called another three people before giving up. It was far less painful to handle on their own than to discover how little people cared. Society had discarded her just as it had discarded her father almost fifty years earlier. Their mother had become a leper in the eyes of all the people the girls had been seeing in their house since they had come back to Pakistan, *their aunties,* women Zaib had loved, her 'friends', some who had known her for more than twenty years. No one wanted to have anything to do with an alcoholic and a woman abandoned by her husband. Devi's husband was posted in Multan for a year so they couldn't ask Devi khala for help either. How little things had changed. The responsibility of taking care of their mother and the house matured them overnight. They took turns to carry out household chores, ordering the meals, keeping the house clean, and paying the bills. They also took turns feeding Zaib. They had to make sure she ate.

Alya got in touch with Dr Rizwi who came over and tried to talk to her. She had screamed at him, 'What the hell is this man doing here? Get him out!'

Every time he came, her reaction was the same. Until finally he told Alya and Sonia, 'I am sorry, but until she is willing to accept help I can't do anything. In fact it could make matters worse. Right now she doesn't even know there is a problem. We can't force anything on her.'

Sonia had looked frustrated and prayed that she would die. That would be better for her.

Their last option was closed. Dr Rizwi was gone for now. And they had ammi to themselves again.

Alya and Sonia continued going to college in the morning and at night they kept checking on Zaib while she slept. During the day they hired a maid to watch her. Sometimes they were delirious and light headed. When they weren't with Zaib they talked and laughed about the most absurd things until their stomachs hurt. It was a time marked by the cusp amid lurid fantasy and the whimsical fascination of dreams, each person in the house strung to their own *truth* about the omnipresent *things* in their lives. Zaib was drifting between daddy and her fairy dreams and her nightmares, between her old mango garden and the emerald green of Zakar's oceans. She picked the shell that most looked like it would have an oyster in it and listened to it for the rest of the day, waiting for the oyster to emerge. Sometimes the matchstickmen stamped on her. That's when daddy arrived to save her and then left again.

The girls too invented new worlds and stories – such great acts of blasphemy and of love in minutes! Fascinating and horrific, all enshrined in a mystical life that they had created for themselves. They even made up a private language to communicate with each other when they were bored. Alya often pretended she was a bird and made flapping motions with her hands, running from room to room and laughing loudly at the slightest sight or sound. Sonia laughed hysterically at her sisters' antics and started making a collage of dried rose petals, stuck together in the shape of a pear. She said she would add other things, like butterfly wings later. She also developed a knack for making fun of the girls in her college by mimicking their expressions and the way they talked. One day the girls decided to commit suicide together. They discussed the details of how to do it, and then started to laugh.

The days were a collection of moments that created a rare mutual respect between the sisters and surrounded them with a nimbus covering their existence as if they were a single entity. That one year passed like several lifetimes and yet when it was all over they regretted losing the *madness* of a time that could only be called an act of providence to bring them together in a bond that could never be broken. They had smiled at a horizon no one else could see. They understood that people touched by extreme trauma often become the spirits of their fantasies; they no longer feel the urgent need to separate fantasy from reality as if their sanity depended on it – unlike the rest. They learnt that that is not what matters in life, what matters is what you have for the people who suffer with you.

Ammi, in her room was with her bits and pieces whispering to her as the days blended into each other.

The tip of his tongue on my palm. I have eaten all the moths in the veranda for night to never come. Did you know that daddy's head is couched inside me to be safe between the wraps of my wisdom in his? His torn pajamas are in the fish bowl with the fish that eat their babies in that way that I was amazed until the bits of stars on your hands jumped into the water giving birth to nymphs so that sailors catch their last breath of the many they love in the sea... while daddy slyly creeps back into my womb to see the beginning of creation spilling blue paint on us humans where lakes of honey washed ashore the sins of generations. I want to put my head on your chest again and pray for the time in a second to speak of your journey when butterflies swam and ants were kind. I wait for your fingers to sweep away the cobwebs stuck to the space between my ear and a sound. In an upside down frenzy he wore my sleeve on one arm to show his love written on the lines of his forehead. Mama, if paintings were all yellow what would a blue bird sing? The door to Ghazala's room is broken now.

ঙ্গ

23

Dead Stars

One night, when it was Alya's turn to guard mummy, she fell asleep. When she woke up Zaib's bed was empty. She panicked. This was what both the sisters had dreaded the most. Alya ran to the bathroom first and found her on the floor with her head face down. She wasn't moving. There was a stream of blood flowing down the slope of the floor towards the opening for the outlet to the gutter. She turned her mother around as quickly as she could. The blood was gushing out of her forehead. Shaking with fear, she picked her mother's head up and put it on her lap. Oh God please don't let her die. She could see her mouth twitching slightly. She wasn't dead. When Sonia saw her she blacked out for a moment. They picked her up and managed to put her in the back seat of the car.

It was 4 a.m. 'Sonia I am sorry I fell asleep. It was my turn.'

'It's not your fault Alya. It really isn't.' They took her to the hospital closest to their house. The hospital staff stitched the cut after looking at both girls suspiciously and after enquiring about where the injured woman's husband (and their father) was. They were interrogating them. 'We don't know,' was all that Sonia said, angry at their insensitivity but also wondering if they could smell the alcohol on Zaib's breath. Later she told Alya, 'If they had known she was drunk, we could all have been in big trouble.'

Four more months passed and Zaib had hardly left her room. The girls fed her easy to swallow mashed food and vegetables in case she choked.

Zaib continued to buy wine, sometimes vodka from her bootlegger. They didn't, rather couldn't stop her, but they found out where Jason, the bootlegger lived. Sonia went to the *basti* where Jason and his family lived. He answered the door. 'Please do not bring that stuff to the house any more, our mother is getting ill.' He stopped, but Zaib found herself another source. One day Alya lost her temper and went into her room and shook her, 'Wake up! Wake up!! Tell me where all the bottles are!' Zaib looked perplexed. Eventually, she found them hidden in various cupboards and boxes –one was under the bed. She went into the bathroom and broke every bottle she found. The house smelled of wine and vodka for the next two days but that night Zaib was sober, after almost three weeks of being drunk. She sat in the lounge looking out of the window. Alya went up to her, nervous after what had happened.

'Ammi are you feeling better?'

'Why, what was wrong with me?'

'Ammi this is the first time in weeks you have been with us like this.' She dared not the word.

'Alya stop being silly, you are exaggerating. I am fine honey.' She smiled the same smile.

When Sonia asked the same question in the evening, Zaib said,

'What's happened to you girls? I am fine. I just like having a drink or two every now and again, that's all. Why is that so bad?'

That night Sonia caught her mother looking at her reflection in the mirror and touching the scar on her forehead from her fall in the bathroom. She looked confused and touched it repeatedly, until she realized someone was watching. She saw Sonia and looked away hurriedly.

Later that night Sonia turned to Alya, 'I think we need to call Dr Rizwi again, we can't handle this ourselves anymore.'

During the next five or six months the girls lived in a state suspended between life and death with Zaib holding on to her existence with the thread of a saint's prayer wrapped in a piece of cloth, she had been told to wear by a *maulvi* the girls had brought to the house one morning when they felt all else had failed. Zaib would remain drunk for days. She would talk in mixed sentences and cry for hours while the girls tried to console her. She said she prayed to God because she believed he loved his children. She said she heard the *azaan* in her sleep and in the morning telling her it would all be all right, telling her that belief and faith are about God and God loves us… 'God does not punish us … God loves us you know'. Then suddenly for no apparent reason she would stop drinking for two or three days at a time and ask about Hassan. She had worked out the fact that he had gone but she still enquired about whether he had contacted them. She didn't seem to know if days or months even years had passed. When she was drunk she hurt herself and when she was sober she didn't remember she was ever drunk. For an outsider it was a glimpse into the lives of three ghost-like creatures that saturated the walls of their house with tears, laughter and anguish. They all tried *together* to save lives and learnt that every day was a blessing. Many years later the girls told their husbands and their grown-up children stories of those strange days.

Dr Rizwi started coming to the house regularly. Alya tried to find out about their father, but no one seemed to have any idea.

In her moments of clarity they saw their old mother back and with the help of Dr Rizwi – who took each day step by step, her moments of sobriety started to become longer and longer. It was a gradual process. Six months later Dr Rizwi told them that she had recovered for all practical purposes though there was a possibility of a relapse. The dread of death had been averted. Alya and Sonia could finally focus on the future.

Now that ammi was better, both girls' thoughts were on abba. They had both secretly believed his absence was temporary, but now they were beginning to worry. In between their chores, in the silence of their beds they wept for him, they craved their father, their Atlas. Where was he? Was he all right? Would they ever see him again? They wished they could talk to him just one more time, they thought if they could have they might have understood things better, they might have put things right.

ઉ૪૭

24

Red Rain

But before they had their mother back, they met Shahid.

Three months before Zaib is sober the house is crawling with laughter. All three beds are empty. No one knows what might happen next and the needle awareness of that knowledge shocks one of the inhabitants of the house into displaying a bizarre euphoric energy, manifesting itself in sporadic bursts of hysterical laughter or loud wailing after a particularly harrowing day at home. Strident animated fixtures revolving about the house disgorge their aversion to the imbalance caused by her. It is not long before Alya, the girl responsible for this violent spillage, quickly returns to normality and the house forgets what just happened, returning to its simple gravity. They see them in awkward moments, when the sun is not following straight lines or when coffee cups have overturned. It is uncertain how the house or the people molded to the inside of it precluded outsiders for so long. Their heaven and their hell were intact.

The two girls anticipate a solid emptiness and dread the cartoon belligerence of their mother, when they are standing in front of her bedroom door. When mummy lets them in without questions they think she has given in, gone insane. When she doesn't they want her to die in her sleep. Either way, they smile their desperate smiles. Her senses are even sharper than a snake's now; she doesn't miss the unintended cruelties of her daughters, so they have to be careful about their kindnesses too…

Usually Zaib would be sleeping or drinking with her bedroom door closed. It had been almost two years since their father had left. The house was dusty. Alya and Sonia had begun revisiting old friends, but their old friends now looked at them oddly as if they knew something the girls didn't. Sonia was not ashamed of her mother. She knew she had a disease. The others didn't care about other people's diseases. They wanted to scrutinize the girls and ask them details about their drunken mother, as if they were convicts on trial. The two girls could see it in the eyes of their friends, the hungry breed that fed on the sores of other people, *later they will go home and tell their heartless mothers the whole story.* They wanted to disassociate themselves with them and meet people who knew nothing about them at all or who didn't care about the sins and misfortunes of others. It had been so long since they had met other people and talked to them they felt as if they had forgotten how to communicate properly. Alya felt nervous even saying hello to other students at college. Sonia hardly ever greeted anyone at college anymore. She avoided conversations in general.

❧

One day Sonia decides to start a conversation with Rafia, a dark skinned, wiry girl at college, who rolls up joints regularly in the bathroom. Sonia knows some other students who smoke weed too. She asks Rafia if she can try some weed. Rafia gives her a few drags and she feels relaxed and light-headed, she asks Rafia if she can buy some. She sells her a small piece about one centimeter thick for 200 rupees and invites Sonia to a party the following weekend to meet the rest of their group. She says it's not really a party, more of a large get-together, where there would be lots of 'dope and booze'. The weekend comes quickly. At the get together everyone is eating hash cakes and hash cookies. The smoke is so dense Sonia can only see the outline of faces.

The room is red and a white ceiling fan laps up music playing in the background. She likes the song, it is the last track on Nina Simone's album 'To Love Somebody' but it doesn't get rid of her nervousness. She searches for a familiar face. At last Rafia sees her. She comes to her languidly, but not without a bright smile on her face. She tells her she is glad Sonia is there.

Sonia sits down on the nearest sofa with a small cluster of students. Some are rolling up; others are looking forward to their next drag as the spliff is passed around the circle, slowly. When it is Sonia's turn she tries to look like as much of a pro as possible. She holds the spliff at a certain angle and tries to appear disinterested in what others may think of her. She inhales deeply and the smoke blurs her vision. She remains talkative and alert so that it is assumed that her system can take the drug in its stride. After the joint finishes she gets up to take a piece of cake. The cake is more potent than the spliff. She is drowning in a land of cushions. Her hands reach out like tentacles in the dark fabric surrounding her. She catches herself in a dilemma about how to reach her feet with her hands in such a small space and so little light. She can just about see the others around her from a hole in the sofa. There are pins in all the things around her and the rest of the twenty or thirty people in the red room, drift from one place to the next, occasionally stopping to make a comment or to flirt with each other. She feels paranoid. People's voices fuse together, falling like blunt instruments. Sonia listens, while her mind fights to rationalize recent events in her life. Someone asks her if she needs anything else. She shakes her head and sinks more deeply into the sofa. The lights become dimmer ... something would have to be done soon about ammi otherwise she would die, they had to take her somewhere forcibly and find a cure ... Alya had to be saved too, she had been through enough as it is ... Did abba miss his daughters and ammi's hugs? She dwindles briefly then clarity returns, only to scatter into the anonymous darkness of lamplight again, seconds later. Behind it all there is an unremitting guilt that nags her to be sober again. What would ammi say? This new sensation of careless contemplation must have a price. People around her continue to swap messages and then dissipate before they can be caught saying that which would grow in forbidden corners after they'd left. Do they know the damage they can cause with a wrong word, or the happiness they are capable of spreading just by saying something kind to someone?

She is still wondering what must be done about ammi, when she is distracted by a man's voice. It is forceful and determined in its tone. Sonia combs the crowd in front of her carefully looking for the voice. She sees a man, a little older than herself talking to a small group of people. She notices that his movements are exaggerated and whatever he is talking about he obviously feels strongly about it. He is striking to look at, about five feet seven inches tall or so, with a slight build and sharp Iranian features. His hair is shoulder length and his complexion light. He also has a French beard. Sonia wants to hear what he is saying but when she tries to get up, she can't. She looks down at her body. One final effort at getting up and she sees him standing in front of her. She can hear her heart beat faster. He smiles knowingly as if he had sensed her interest.

'I thought I'd introduce myself since I haven't met you here before. I'm Shahid.'

Sonia can hardly form the words to make a clear reply, all she can say is 'Sonia'.

He is suddenly sitting on the cushion next to her and telling her about the benefits of taking drugs. He is talking about hallucinations and how drugs can be used as a form of enlightenment and a source of inspiration. He is so close now, she is slightly uncomfortable almost feels his breath on her face.

'The world can be divided into as many things or parts as you want it to. It's just that with the naked mind you can only see what you have been conditioned to see. Drugs free your mind and they take your inhibitions away.'

'But they can also kill you.'

'Not if you know how to take them. Why do you think they grow naturally as plants? What could be more "pure"? They are not meant to be abused but they can alter your life by helping you see things in a new light and that is what life is all about, it has to be. You just have to know how to use them in the right way.'

'Besides, you never know,' he went on to quote Alduous Huxley, 'Maybe this world is another planet's hell.' He laughs out loud. 'Now that was a great man and a genius.'

He seems intelligent, different at the least, even if she doesn't agree with everything he is saying. She just nods. He is looking at Sonia with concentrated interest to gauge her reactions.

Two weeks later Sonia met him at another get together. He got up from where he was sitting and came across the room to meet her.

'So have you tried something yet?' He smiled.

'No, and I am not going to either. I know what drugs can do to a person.'

'So I suppose you'll just have to watch while I do them then!'

She shrugged. She was not stoned this time. 'I am sorry I didn't ask you where you study the last time we met. I was a bit out of it, you know.'

'I don't. I gave up after school, I don't believe in it. My parents don't agree, but they can hardly win the argument. They just have to look at themselves, going through the motions, living their banal lives, and the answer is staring them squarely in the face.'

'So what will you do now?'

'What does anyone do? Do you think an investment banker has a better life just because he or she is an investment banker? Sonia, life is so full of possibilities. I'll go travelling and see the world.'

There was something unreal about him. Maybe it was his adolescent idealism; maybe it was just that he fitted the picture too well. Nevertheless, she liked his honesty and his courage to say what he thought despite other people's opinion of him. He scoffed at them. His ideas were original and thought provoking for a man of his age. Sonia had not come across a person with such beliefs before and she started looking forward to their conversations. They met frequently at parties. She met his best friend, Salman at one of them. Shahid introduced him as 'his best friend and worst enemy'. They were unusually familiar, but being around them Sonia got the feeling they were in constant competition. They were constantly offensive to each other, yet it was apparent that they knew each other so well they could finish off each other's sentences and read what the other was going to say before he said it. It was their strange intimacy that made Sonia uncomfortable. Shahid was like a stranger to her again. Salman told Sonia, Shahid was 'a fake'. 'He pulls it off so well, doesn't he? He's really just like the rest of us, probably worse.' Shahid raised his eyebrows. 'You know me better and better, what a genius you are Salman!' They had their own language, their own codes and it disconcerted her, but strangely it also made him more intriguing.

'So what's it all about then?' she asked him.

'Nothing in particular,' he said, 'it is what you do with the things you appreciate in the world that matters.'

'Shahid, don't you think your family is hurt when you take drugs and stuff? I mean you must feel answerable to them.'

'No, why should I? I didn't ask to be born; besides, parents want us to live out their dreams. Why should we be pawns in their little messed-up games?'

'That is so cynical.'

'To be honest, they are just middle-class people with middle-class ideas.'

She felt uneasy about bringing the subject up. After meeting a few more times, he told her, 'Most people are so boring, I can hardly wait to get away from them. I never tire of being around you. You seem to emanate peace.'

They started to meet almost everyday, inventing new ideas about the world and trying to devise fresh plans for changes that would make individuals more fulfilled and the world a kinder place to live in. They discussed different forms of anarchy, even socialism but nothing seemed to work except in theory. They both believed that in a capitalist state the entire population suffered from enforced ignorance and they read Chomsky together. People were being mass-produced like things – by large conglomerates and fancy universities like Harvard, as if they were commodities. 'We must not become mincemeat like all those other unfortunate people who don't even know what is happening to them. They are stupefied.' Once she told him he was too idealistic, he said, 'Sonia you can't have it both ways. Either you believe in something and you try and change things or you follow the rest. Look what's happening here. We are collapsing as well. Why do you think that is?' Then one day he asked her about her parents. Her short reply was that they were separated and ammi was ill most of the time in her bedroom. Shahid didn't probe.

As she started spending more time with him, Sonia thought he understood her better than anyone ever had and she trusted him with her.

꧁꧂

Alya and Sonia were in bed at night. Alya asked Sonia what she would do if Shahid left her.

'Nothing, I would try and find someone else, but it is something I'd rather not think about because I love him so much.'

'Do you really think you are suited to each other?'

'Yes, I do. He is special.'

Sonia respected and admired Shahid's intelligence and she listened to his ideas with interest, but she thought it was a shame that he didn't want to study any further. She told him he could 'reach great heights' if he did. His standard reply was that *success* was a relative term. Sonia said nothing mattered when there was no food on the table. 'If that happened you would forget all your ideals in an instant and go and serve at tables if you had to.' She talked about him to Alya at length, telling her how different he was, though a bit too much of an idealist. 'You know I don't think I could actually marry him, but who knows.' Alya looked relieved.

'Although he rarely convinces me to change my opinions he is definitely challenging to speak to!'

'You should be some sort of healer,' he said to Sonia over and over again. She encouraged him to put his ideas on paper saying they were original and interesting. He seemed proud of himself, when he was with her. Gradually he spent more time at the house. He told Sonia how unhappy he was at home and frequently slept over at their place in the spare bedroom. Alya, Shahid and Sonia often talked until the early hours of the morning, until neither of them could keep awake. Sometimes they fell asleep together on the bed and they'd wake up huddled together in one corner of the bed.

Within weeks he was an indelible part of their lives and Alya began to look forward to their meetings as much as Sonia did. If he arrived before her sister did from college, Alya and he would talk for hours. He'd hold her hand if she was depressed, he'd soothe her, tell her it would be alright, that things would look up eventually and all this would be behind them. At times he would stroke her hair, comfort her, she'd put her head in his lap and he'd cradle her to sleep.

Devi was back in town after being in Multan for almost a year. During her husband's posting there she had only been to Lahore for a brief visit just after Hassan had left Zaib. She came to visit one weekend. It was a rare occurrence now. Most of her day, Devi now, spent in prayer.

Devi had seen Shahid a few times in the house. Sonia had told her they were *in love*. In return, Devi had smiled and pinched her cheek. But this time she saw him again for the third time in one month. She asked Alya why he sleeps over so often.

'He sleeps here everyday with us of course auntie, where else is he going to sleep? He is miserable at home with his crazy parents.'

'Sonia, please ensure that the respect of your family remains intact. At least I can trust you to uphold the values of this family, plus his problems with his parents are for them to solve, not you.' Sonia felt sorry for her and at the same time ashamed of her own weakness, but the time for judgment was over. Now everyone took what they could.

'Khala we can't be so cruel and send him back there. And I really love him. Maybe we will get married one day.'

And before she knew it, it came out automatically, as if without thought.

'Khala you knew about my sister, didn't you?'

'Knew what?'

'About what was happening with Asad bhai. They were in your house locked in *his* room. You knew.'

'They were just talking.'

'Why didn't you do anything? How could you let it go khala? How could you do it to her? She was just a child.'

Devi turned around and walked away without uttering a word.

☙❧

One afternoon Devi came to visit again, unexpectedly. Sonia was in college. First she went in to see her sister in her bedroom. Zaib was asleep. She checked her breathing and left the room.

'Sakina, where are the girls?' Sakina, the middle-aged maid, who always looked worried and generally uneasy shifted uncomfortably, '*Baaji*, please stop this boy from coming to the house. He brings trouble.' Devi almost pushed passed her.

'Alya, it's me, open the door!'

She banged on Alya's bedroom door.

'I am coming!'

She opened the door looking worn. 'What's wrong?'

'Where is that boy? Alya, where is he?'

They found him in the storeroom, trying to open the lock of Zaib's jewellery cupboard. Devi barged in on him.

'How dare you, you thief. I always knew you were trouble. Get out of my sister's house now!'

Shahid seemed unmoved and smiled nonchalantly.

'Ok ok keep it cool auntie. I am leaving.'

He looked back at Alya as he walked out.

Alya ran to her, 'Devi khala, please let it go.'

'What do you mean, he is a thief!'

'I love him.'

'But I thought he was ...'

She didn't let her finish, 'I can't live without him.'

'What is wrong with you Alya, you know how your sister feels about him.'

'I can't help it.'

That evening Sonia came home late from college.

Alya ran to her, 'They are sending him away.' Her face was red.

'Who is sending who away?'

'I don't know what to do. Sonia I am sorry. But Devi khala is going to kick him out. She found him taking something from the storeroom. We can't let him go.'

Sonia's eyes were stone cold. She was quiet for a moment. 'I don't care for him much anyway, anymore. Just let it be, Alya. Let it be. Just let him go. We obviously didn't know him at all.'

'Sonia, please don't do this to me.'

Sonia saw the guilt in her sister's eyes – and the desperation – but she said nothing.

Neither girl ever mentioned Shahid to the other again. A few days after he had left, Shahid came back to Alya in her dreams ... the night he had kissed her, the way he had cupped her face in his hands gently and told her he would be there to take care of things. The next morning she had barely been able to leave her bed and dreaded seeing her sister. They hardly spoke to each other after he left but it didn't last long.

Both sisters knew why they had succumbed to a stranger so easily and why in the 'madness' of a vaporous time they were ready to give up everything that was most important to them so quickly. But it taught them that there was little space between what they had and what they could lose and so the remnants of that time remained for a while, luckily not long enough.

☙❧

One morning Zaib called them both into her bedroom, soon after Dr Rizwi had told them she was out of danger for now.

'I wanted to talk to you about abba.'

'Ammi it's ok, he will come back.'

'No, Alya I have to try and find him. I have to know where he is.'

And that was it. Nothing could be done about it. They discouraged her but she was adamant and started making enquiries. She found out that he had left the city a week after leaving home.

☙

25

Love

Mummy had even looked for Zaib in the closets. She was hiding again.

'Rashida! Sharifa! Go and look for her, she must be somewhere here; she's just being difficult as usual. Tell her, the guests are arriving.' Mummy had organized a lavish birthday party for Zaib's thirteenth birthday.

She had told her the week before 'this is a very special birthday, after this you will become a young lady, Zaib. You will be expected to come out in society.' Zaib was starting to feel more grown up already. She had told mummy she wanted a dollhouse. 'Like the one's they sell abroad.' Of course mummy had bought it for her, a spectacular dollhouse with carpeted rooms and weighty furniture.

The lounge had been cleared out and the ceiling was covered with balloons of all colours. Streamers descended. Prism rain. The children of the most influential people in Lahore had been invited. Mummy had told Zaib four times that the Chief Justice's grand children were also attending as if she didn't understand the first time. They were about to arrive and Zaib was supposed to be on her best behaviour and in her best clothes but Zaib was missing from the house and mummy was losing her patience. All the servants were ordered to look in different rooms. Each of the ten bedrooms was searched thoroughly. They looked in the bathrooms, the storerooms, the pantry, the washrooms, even on the roof. Zaib could not be found. She had crossed all limits this time! Mummy was furious.

By this time the Chief Justice's grandchildren had arrived too. Their mother had asked to see the birthday girl. Mummy had to make an excuse and the woman went, leaving her well-dressed children behind. Mummy asked one of the maids to entertain the children while she would go and look for her daughter herself. Nobody had checked the garden yet, so she went outside, holding up her silk *shalwar* in case she got mud on it.

'Zaib! Zaib!'

Then she remembered, she might be with that damn menace, Ghazala; she hadn't checked, the servant's quarter where Ghazala and her family lived. She had tried so hard to get rid of Ghazala but it hadn't worked. She walked up to the door of her quarter, trying not to let her clothes brush against the door. She opened it, without knocking. Nothing registered initially. Her first memory of that moment was seeing an old, faded sheet, once belonging to her, spread out on the floor. The yellow print had almost merged with the background cream and blue of the sheet. When it became too frayed and old to be used in the house, she had given it to Ghazala's father instead of throwing it away. She saw Zaib lying on the old sheet, on her back, with her head in Ghazala's lap. Ghazala was caressing her face dotingly, smoothing her lips with her fingers softly. Mummy walked out of the room quietly and then returned. 'Zaib,' she said with a steady voice, 'please come outside.'

Zaib jumped up, Ghazala ran past mummy, out of the room, vanishing into thin air. Zaib could see stars in the sweltering space around her and her head started spinning.

'Your friends have arrived. They are waiting for you.' Her voice was unusually calm.

ଓଃ

26

Solitude

Those you love kill you a little everyday.

Hassan lived alone in a two-bedroom apartment in Karachi, overlooking the sea. The walls were crisp white icing on a cake; he was the first to see the smooth, un-creased walls of its shining newness and brush his fingers across the infinite little dots of its invincible spine. It was daunting. Stark creaminess of fresh paint bedazzled him. The medicinal smell of it made him nauseous. He had chosen to spend the rest of his time here, in a new apartment because it was devoid of any mistrust or tragedy, it proclaimed its unerring loyalty to himself and the consciousness of no one but the one's who built it. One of the reasons that Hassan chose Karachi after he left Zaib was that no one he knew lived there; the other was the sea. He found a job through his contacts with a local firm that paid him enough to live modestly. That was good enough for him.

The dense pollution of the city betrayed the coexistent splendour of its ocean. Hassan tried to stay away from the more polluted areas as much as possible. He was afraid of the hostility of such places. He met no one but the people he worked with and came home with a few vegetables and a chicken or a pound of meat everyday. While cooking he looked out at the sea from his kitchen window. Only his Zaib was more beautiful. He missed the cadence of her body, the sound of blood through her veins. Without her, he came home to an emptiness that locked him inside it.

Initially, her absence was a small blessing. The unique peace that comes with solitude is welcomed, for a time. Barely two months had passed and he started looking for her in every street corner, behind all the shops that she may have liked for one reason or another. He looked in the fish markets she had nightmares about and the church gardens that would have enchanted her. In the evenings when he came back from work he noticed the absence of a voice that told him he was the most loved man in the world. His throat would go dry thinking about how far away his lovely wife was. His actions in the last few months sickened him, when he thought about how he had abandoned Zaib he lost the will to wake up the next day, but when he did, and on a brighter day, he realized the sad flamboyance of dreams and memories. He was no artist but he knew that the collapse of reality in the face of a single longing was the greatest failure of the human mind, and that's when he remembered Zaib as a mere mortal.

Daily he would complete the circle unsuccessfully. Where was she now? Without her, he could scarcely define who he was. How could he retrieve all that was gone, life wasn't big enough. When he looked for the reasons to stay or to go back, he realized his actions in the last few months had left him no choice. He remembered Zaib quoting Omar Khayyam, 'The moving finger writes, and having writ, Moves on, nor all your piety nor wit, Can lure it back to cancel half a line, Nor all your tears wash out a word of it.' He had been condemned by his own actions.

଼

In Pakistan her old friends had stopped meeting her. They didn't want to be associated with the scandal. No one accepted a former drunk and a woman who had lost her husband. They had too much to lose in a society that judged people by what others said. Her friends were burying themselves in the walls of her proliferating home, one by one, their hollow laughter filling her house with fake mirth. She had to go before they returned again. Daddy was gone, Ghazala was dead, her father no longer laughed his laugh and mummy was lost to the stars. The girls were grown up and could look after themselves. So one day, just like that, she told her daughters she was leaving.

'I have been in touch with a few old friends in Zakar. You both know the scandal in Pakistan is too much for me to bear. I don't want to meet any of those people anymore and if I live here I won't survive. Girls, I will make sure you have tickets to come and see me as often as you want. You can also write to me and talk to me on the phone. You have this house and I will send you enough money every month and keep checking on you. Please don't be upset with me. I love you both so much, but I just have to go from here right now. I will keep coming back, this will always be home.'

And that was it. The girls had no idea what was coming, and before they could question her, she was gone. It was so much like ammi…

Zaib visited the dunes over and over again looking for the same anthills that were her temple years ago. Now all she found were the delicate footprints of invisible ants lacing the dunes, before they melted away. In them she saw bits of the last year, the smell of a soiled *shalwar*, the curse of an unknown face and at times Ralph, who found her vodka bottles for her when they were missing. Now, even more, she had difficulty in separating her dreams from her reality. There was nothing insignificant about either, yet she startled herself with the inability to ask the bigger question: how important was it? Was it in God's design to make us see such clear definitions in things that relate only to our minds and nothing outside of them? We were not omnipresent; we were persistently scraping away that from the world, which seemed real to us, leaving behind the inner core, that which wasn't. It was impossible to ask an objective viewer because there wasn't one and so the question became imperative for Zaib. She had to find out.

During her procrastinations she reached bizarre conclusions far beyond her expectations, sometimes she arrived at conclusions that made living unnecessary and therefore the worry about reality and fantasy didn't exist. Then again it negated life. There was no logic to it, just the emotional attachments to Alya, Sonia, Hassan, and her Devi. She would have to leave them all behind if she decided to go, that would be hard but maybe this was worse for them. She found herself thinking about death more often. Ghazala was waiting for her, of that she was certain. Death defied death. She thought about why Hassan had left. She couldn't blame herself because if she did she would have to re-invent everything she believed in. He had tried to stop her from living the way she wanted to. *He* had changed just like her father said he would, she hadn't. That is why after five years without Hassan, she had to try and find him again. Her last attempt before moving to Zakar had failed but now it had to be done. She wanted him to know that she was still the same even now and she wouldn't stay if he really didn't want her to, she just wanted to see him, she wanted to look at his hands, his eyes so that she knew for sure that all those years with him had happened the way she had seen them. *He* had misunderstood her. Then one day she got a phone call from a friend. She told her they had found an address where Hassan was living in Karachi. She was going to see him at last. She wanted to scream. For the first time in five years she felt safe.

The next day she was on a flight to Karachi. She forgave him. She had so much to tell him, her daddy whom she had slept with all those nights she couldn't touch him. Her daddy, she held onto when the days were too long and bleak to get through. She wanted to say she was sorry: things could be the same again, like the old days! She wished she could fly to him and be with him that instant. Her friend, Uzma, drove her to the block of apartments Hassan lived in. On the way she stuck her head out of the window like a child, craning her neck to see his world. There was definitely something magical about it, that's why he chose this place! They arrived at the block of flats, *his* block of flats. She started climbing the stairs, her legs weak. Every expression of his, every movement and twitch of his body rested on her quivering hands. As she got closer her heart started beating faster. *Daddy I am here.* She knocked on *his* door.

❧

The last time Sonia and Alya had gone to see Zaib in Zakar was just after she had come back from Karachi. 'The accident' took place the first night they were there. They had woken up to find several broken bottles of sleeping pills on her dressing table. The doctor said she was lucky she had survived after taking so many pills.

He asked what had happened. Alya told him.

'Does her sister know? Can she be called?'

They rang Devi.

'You know, I have had enough. I am so tired. Sometimes I wish it would all just be over.' Alya was sobbing.

'Alya, don't, please stop it. Don't even say it.' Sonia hadn't slept for days.

'Aren't you tired of this constant torture?'

'What will we do without her? Imagine how she is feeling.'

They went to sleep, each, thinking about why God was doing this to their family. They thought about life without mummy, but then what was the use, she would come back again, dead or alive. Memories singe your life.

'Zaib, are you still in pain?'

Zaib was somewhere else....

Around me the white hospital room tells me that I am now living in a cardboard box. There are no birds or ants here with me, I am alone. They have lost me on their important journey, yet I have seen them all, night after night in this room with me, while I slept, but now they have abandoned me. Hassan stood in the doorway, morning after morning holding tea in his hands and waiting for me patiently to emerge from this stupor that has stayed with us for so long. I cannot disappoint him anymore. In this dim light of dawn, when the nurses have given me their last smile as a token, I know that in my father's garden, at home in Pakistan, there will be crows waiting to hear what I have to say to my sister and what she has to say to me, but today they will miss our morning conversation. Is it morning now? Today they will be ignorant of our chat and we will not see them, it may be our last chance. My daughters are home, sleeping. I can see them in bed. They are resting. Devi is touching my sheet. I have no love for these doctors and nurses. I feel sorry for my family. Devi is praying, I can see that from the way she is holding on to my sheet, she keeps her mouth shut so she thinks I don't know what she is doing. It is her habit because she thinks I am really an atheist. I will let her believe it. I will wait until she has finished. Then I'll ask her what God has told her.

They discharged Zaib from the hospital two days later.

❧

It was five years since Hassan had moved to Karachi. There wasn't a day he didn't think about Zaib. He wanted to call her, but as time passed it became harder. His shame became too deep. But he kept track of her secretly and knew that she had recovered and was living in

Zakar by then. Still he couldn't go back, he couldn't undo these years or her tears.

And then it ended, abruptly like walking into a bus, without a past or a present, as if life never happened. He may have been in the middle of a thought, or studying the pattern on his curtains, no one would know. He died a couple of days before Zaib knocked on his door in Karachi. It was a heart attack, the doctors said; he went to sleep one night and never woke up. The neighbours found him in the morning. In his room on the mantelpiece there was a photograph of Zaib sitting at the edge of a table. She was trying to balance herself and she had her arms outstretched towards the camera. He talked to it on days when it didn't threaten his sanity.

When they found him he lay, flattened out, a stingray to be dissected and tested. On his bedside table there was a small blue lamp, still switched on when they found him; he had never liked sleeping in the dark. At the foot of the bed, his shoes were placed neatly together and in his cupboard there were six shirts and four pairs of trousers almost identical. Sonia flew to Karachi the morning after ammi found out he was dead. Ammi was staying at her cousin Vinny's house. She was sleeping when Sonia arrived.

Vinny told Sonia she had been sedated. Sonia's eyes were swollen and bloodshot.

'What did she do when she found out?'

'She said nothing all day and then lit a match to herself. Luckily she has only suffered first-degree burns. The doctor says she will recover with some minor scarring.'

Sonia couldn't stop pacing the room where her mother slept. She didn't have time to think about mourning the loss of her father, yet. When Zaib finally woke up, Sonia almost ran to her.

'Oh Sonia, what a surprise! Why didn't you tell me you were coming.' Zaib seemed oblivious to what had happened, cheerful even.

'Is Alya alright?'

'Yes mum, she is fine. Daddy had a heart attack. They have already told you, haven't they?' She was deliberately brutal.

'They told me daddy was gone. I was knocking on his door and his neighbour told me, daddy was gone. He has actually gone, I know that.' She looked at her hands with concentration, but smiled all the same. 'He is in heaven.'

Sonia wished she wasn't alone with her mother.

That night Sonia sat with her mother's head in her lap all night.

Where is he?

When I knew daddy had gone I lost my sense of physical being. My body had no face or form. I felt no sensation, just a vague perception of the objects surrounding me. They held capsules of information, that gave me an idea of what they were, but they had no relation to one another, they were merely random materials surviving independently of my will and sense. My senses spread across the room without my consent. My head is in Sonia's lap. She is worried about me and I am sick of me. I know I will never see daddy again, but I am not sure why. I am asleep...

(The bed is breathing with ants. If you look closely you can see her buried beneath them, a wriggling wound below the head. God looks down, pale, dismayed, regal and perfect. She reaches out to him but her hands are tied. She thinks of Gulliver. His familiar face is a comfort. Her body starts to itch. Her neck is wet from where the skin has been peeled off. The ants are building a home in her hair, her nails, warm in her womb bed. Mother ant. A few minutes ago they attacked her nibbling quickly, efficiently, alive with the taste of flesh. They form groups of two and three on her stomach, scrutinizing the minutest details of her body, discussing surreptitiously where to go next, what to take, what to leave behind. She watches them with concentration. They had always fascinated her. A new breeze blows across her bed and hundreds of clouds float into the room. They wrap themselves around her and she wishes they'd stay. The ants are suddenly lost and ant land dissipates. Have they forgotten her lifting their little bodies, when they were sprawled at the banks of salvation? She didn't let them drown then. What would they do for her now?)

❧

27

White

Alya turned to Devi, 'Brian is dead.' She paused, 'I remember him so clearly. I remember how she looked at him.'

'I am glad I didn't know him.'

'What will we do now?'

'Wait and see.'

Alya thought of his warmth, his smile and her feelings of jealousy towards him when she was a child – the few times she had seen him in the house. She had inkling about him at that time. There was something there. She had sensed something about how Zaib had felt for him all those years ago.

The bed creaked. It was time. Zaib opened her eyes.

Alya looked closely at her. 'Ammi?'

She looked straight at Alya.

'Alya I want to talk to you.'

Alya walked over to her nervously, looking at her with new eyes.

'Please forgive me.'

'Ammi I love you, forgive you for what?'

'For everything I have put you through.'

And for the first time Alya wanted to tell her about Asad.

Alya turned away, tears streamed down her cheeks. The time had passed for all that.

When Dr Rizwi arrived he called the two girls in to his office.

'She remembers everything this time and she is much better now, but you know such episodes will re-occur, you have to be prepared for that. For the moment, let her do what she wants. She says she wants to go back to Zakar and spend some time alone with her sister. If that's what she wants to do just let her do it.'

'She didn't tell me that's what she wants.'

It was decided.

The following week Zaib and Devi boarded a plane for Zakar.

☙❧

I saw the sloping wizard of moon prisms searching for belligerent plumes in swervy locks on children's prettiness and carpet green garden tops, a sad proclamation of not having a reason or knowing all things with God looking at me in such emblem ways to say I will have no such pleasures that might take place in the middle of life and death I didn't hear her sing for many years after her death. Her emotion came first. Ghazala is dead. Aliya tries to keep a trust eaten by the bowel of her adored disciple... she stretches for clinking pasts, now buried in minds cluttered with signs telling them it's time to go beyond this and find the greater nothingness that surrounds them... she seeps in places of quiet solitude weary and strung to the green dark that Zaib sweeps with her golden hands and goes for mummy's unmasked need to live in water blood and lily loves. They come again, the ghosts and times and apple mummy in pure white as daddy smiles in spring blossoms and takes her to the subtle sea.

The pot was empty when she came to collect the ashes of an urn lost to islands long ago. We are less ready to accept the truth than the lovely things people make up for less than we die to talk about and in the meantime bloodless crows follow angels right to the end.

☙❧

28

Zaib's Judgement

It was Devi's sixth visit to her sister. After Hassan's death Zaib had been in Zakar for a year. Devi picked up a book lying on the glass table in front of her and opened it. She had read it as a young girl – *Great Expectations*. On the inside of the front cover, someone had written a note in blue ink. It said: *For my dearest Zaib, who lives in my heart eternally,* signed, *Brian*. She looked at Zaib; there was still so much about her sister she didn't know.

'Zaib, do you want to sit up and look out of the window, remember those pink crabs you loved so much. They are on their way, it's almost six o'clock.'

Devi watched her anxiously.

They were facing the beach.

'He has left me Devi and now you know he won't come back. Where is God now? The girls want me to go back to that house in Lahore. I can't. I can't do it.'

'Zaib, we all have to go one day. But he is in a better place.'

'You are so damn sure, aren't you? How can you be so certain?'

'Zaib, stop torturing yourself. It isn't your fault.'

'If I hadn't driven him away … I am mad, aren't I? I was always mad. Why didn't mummy just kill me! I was always the bad one.'

'She adored you Zaib. You thought it was I, but it was always you for both of them, all along. I had to leave home to be loved.'

'Devi, you will help me, won't you?'

'How?'

'You know how.'

She read her eyes. 'No, Zaib I can't.'

Devi sat down looking out at the sea. She skimmed through the Oxford years, and their lonely nights, the long walks she took to the park and back and the brooding trees of Hampstead Heath she visited when she occasionally went to London; they were etched on her mind like a Monet on a sunny day. She remembered her friends, long gone, but not forgotten. They probably had families and full lives with interesting jobs, while she waited at home, for her broken son and her husband to return from his new bed. The whole exercise was futile, yet she had to have the strength to survive all this and more for the sake of her faith. She had stopped questioning the fairness of it all. It was not about that now. She thought about her sister and whenever she did her father's face would smile at her, even in her mind, they were not apart. What would he have said now? He knew Zaib better than anyone else. What would he say? What would he say? She wished she could speak to him just once more. Was it time or would she recover? Maybe this time even he wouldn't know, maybe this time he wouldn't help her either. *Oh Zaib please don't ask me.*

'Devi?'

'Give me some time.'

'You love me and you know my life is pointless without him. Don't you?'

'Zaib, would you do it for me?'

'Yes, I would.'

'How can you be so certain?'

'I want you to be content, at least, especially if I had your faith.'

The next day, they talked about other things, like the weather in Zakar and the artificial air of air conditioners being unhealthy for them. After that they laughed about the things they saw and did years before their husbands and their children. Lunch was lobster, because it was Zaib's favourite. At dinner they reminisced and giggled like little girls again. Zaib was still prone to putting her palm under her chin when she listened to her sister, as if making a note of her every expression and gesture. Devi tried to recall all the things that happened in England.

'Did I ever tell you about Mrs Harbottle?'

'No, Devi go on.' She was getting impatient.

'She was such an excellent teacher, but she looked like a man. I swear she wore suits. At the time I didn't understand properly, but now I know she was actually a MAN!'

It was something about the way Devi said the word, 'MAN' that got Zaib laughing uncontrollably. She laughed and laughed, until the tears streamed down her face.

'Please Devi stop, I can't take anymore!' She rocked backwards and forwards holding her stomach.

'She even farted in front of us once.' And that did it. They couldn't stop for another ten minutes.

Zaib turned to her sister, 'There will never be a time better than this for me, please Devi.'

'Zaib, just one more day.'

'Not another minute. Just a second, what time is it?'

'Five.'

'The *azaan*. Just let me hear the *azaan*.'

The doctor came to see Zaib that night. Devi was sitting on her bed, stroking her sister's hair, looking out of the window at the vast blue sea, counting stars in a sky she could not see. Zaib had returned to infancy in sleep, pink with her fairies and no memory. Devi brushed her hand across Zaib's forehead. She thought she saw the familiar curl of her sister's lip, just before the ocean folded outside.

☙❧

29

Alya

Alya woke up lying on her stomach.

Sajid, her husband was still sleeping. He looked so confident even in his sleep. His head was tilted upwards, his chin comfortably perched on the pillow. His features were chiseled, almond-shaped eyes etched in stone. Sajid had given her so much in these last few years. She felt a rush of affection for him.

It was at least ten minutes before he woke up.

'Do you think Pakistan will really collapse? This terrible terrorist nation!'

'No. It can't last, this can potentially cause a world war. America will have to back off at some point. They've done enough damage.'

'What will we do Sajid?'

'What option do we have? We love this damn place, don't we? We will brave it out as best we can.'

She looked up at him, a glint of anxiousness floated in her eyes.

'We've gone beyond that point Alya. We live with the millions who also feel alone and lost, there are no certainties either way.'

Alya glanced at herself in the mirror. She saw the resemblance more and more. The war outside was waging.

She recalled one of the last conversations she had with Devi, not long before ammi's death. It had made perfect sense now. Ammi's *jigsaw puzzle life* made more sense now: the pieces seemed to fit well after her death.

'Devi khala I always wanted to ask you something. What happened to Ghazala? I mean how did she die?'

'She didn't.'

'What?!'

'She didn't die.' Devi had sighed deeply.

'Mummy wanted to protect Zaib from her. Your nani had no choice but to ask her and her father to leave. Of course she couldn't have told Zaib.'

Alya had stood there stone still. She couldn't find her voice for a moment. She couldn't feel her legs. *They'd killed her*. 'How could they do that to her? Her mother destroyed her! She was right all along. And just because she was a servant's daughter?'

'It was for her own sake. Who knows if it was the right decision, but mummy thought it was.'

'Do you have any idea what her supposed death did to ammi? Do you even have a clue? And you whom she loves so much, you didn't tell her! How could you, khala?'

'Well, I think you are old enough to know. Mummy thought they had some sort of sexual feelings towards each other.'

'So bloody what!? How could she betray her like that!'

'She thought she was corrupting Zaib. Maybe she was right.'

Corrupting. Interesting choice of word. How corrupt had Devi's life been? How many lies did she live out everyday?

Alya had turned to Sajid. 'I wonder if she is still alive. Do you think we should try and contact her?'

She had read his mind. 'You are right. It's too dangerous.'

She didn't have the courage to do it.

'Sajid?'

'Hmm?'

'I wish I had tried to find her when we still had time, when ammi was with us. We are part of the betrayal. Do you think it would have made a difference? Do you think I should tell Sonia?'

'Alya she is in a better place. Don't you think we should let it be now?'

She looked outside from their bedroom window. It must have been barely six o'clock in the morning. As she pushed thoughts of ammi away, her attention was back on the road. Most of the people she saw were fruit vendors, truck drivers, milkmen, a few scantily-clad children dragged themselves along as well, some of them carrying younger children in their laps. They must be the poor child beggars or child labourers forced to give up their lives by the time they could barely start walking. She imagined rashy-red faced Afghani children rummaging through the yellow dustbin across the road from her house for food and other odds and ends they could sell, such as paper, polythene bags and pieces of cardboard; a sight she was familiar with. Unfortunately, the rashy-red boys and girls were so far away right now, there was no comfort from their little faces, she wished she could touch them, feel their little pink cheeks on her hands, tell them that they haven't been forgotten, tell them that they don't have to pay for others mistakes or for the blood rivers of those they didn't even know in a land of lost souls. How far would they have gone by now? Could she find them somehow, somewhere in this vast space that no one could any longer call their own? Were they the only displaced lot or was she also one of them – those poor silent children that she ached for, those caught in a rancid loneliness they carried with them on their troubled journey. By now they must be back in their houses, she thought, busy settling their baby brothers and sisters, breaking the backs of moths in their soaking tents, in their 'jhoogees'. How could she reach them ... how she wished she could reach them.

'I don't want to leave this place – ever. I love it here.'

He kissed the top of her head.

'Time for breakfast!'

He left the room.

Alya saw ammi resting on the shores of Zakar's beach. Her head is tilted to the side, her eyes brimming with excitement.

'Ghazala, should we try and swim to the other side?'

Ghazala is running across the beach in a huge white *kurt*a, clearly too big for her; she laughs out loud. 'We are on the other side! We just have to make it back now.' She is waving her hands in the air, the caress of the sun on her.

'We can do it, we can do anything together, can't we Ghazala?'

They were two fish, the murmur of waves between them. Alya closed her eyes tightly and smiled. White foam licked the beach with its effulgent crust. Water flowers fell from a bleached sky. Their hands were locked into each other's. It was finally time to go.

ఆఔ

Acknowledgments

I would like to thank my courageous father, Zulfiqar Ali for his incredible journey. Without him this story would have been incomplete and indeed impossible to write. I could not have done this without immense encouragement, advice and support from Gina Ali at every step, the deepest care, love and patience of Sharmene Ali, and inspiration from Amber Ali who made me see light in my darkest days. Thanks also for the tender love of my sweet Shehryar Ali. Thank you to those friends of mine who walked with me on this tumultuous journey and kept me at bay, Raza Rumi, Iffat Idris, Yasmeen Qazi, Vincent Ioos, Sophie Ioos and Uzma Tariq Haroon. My gratitude to my friends Yasir Masud and Imrana Niazi for their help and encouragement. Thanks to Nighat and Nusrat who endured me at my worst with great bravery! My mentor and the first editor of my poems who made me have faith in myself and who held my hand all the way, Dave Ward, my deepest love and gratitude to him. Thanks to my Editor at Roli Books, Neelam Narula for her wonderful help with *Blue Dust*. My ocean love and thanks to the little pieces of my heart that make each step forward possible, Raza Rashid, Shahmir Rashid, and Rafay Rashid and to my soul mate Salman Rashid, whose hand remains in mine and who took me back to my fairies before it was too late.